CHOSEN BUT SILENCED:

the journey to my voice

LINDSY LOU CUMMINGS

Chosen But Silenced

Trilogy Christian Publishers A Wholly Owned Subsidary of Trinity Broadcasting Network

2442 Michelle Drive Tustin, CA 92780

Rights Department, 2442 Michelle Drive, Tustin, CA 92780.

Trilogy Christian Publishing/TBN and colophon are trademarks of Trinity Broadcasting Network.

Cover design by: JP Staggs

For information about special discounts for bulk purchases, please contact Trilogy Christian Publishing.

Trilogy Disclaimer: The views and content expressed in this book are those of the author and may not necessarily reflect the views and doctrine of Trilogy Christian Publishing or the Trinity Broadcasting Network.

10 9 8 7 6 5 4 3 2 1

Library of Congress Cataloging-in-Publication Data is available.

ISBN: 979-8-89041-381-9

E-ISBN: 979-8-89041-382-6

Dedication

I dedicate this book first and foremost to Yahweh; I pray that this testimony helps bring freedom to the captives of trauma and that they will live out their destinies and enter into Your gates with a peace and gladness they have never known. I also want to thank my beautiful mother for saying yes when everyone wanted her to say no, for leaving that clinic, and for giving me a chance to live a life and to have a voice; I am eternally grateful. To my sisters for making my childhood amazing! Last but certainly not least, to my beautiful husband, Robby, and my amazing children, Brianna, Ethan, Malaki, and Isaiah. For loving me through my pain and standing by me always, for giving me strength to endure and a hope for the future! I love you more than words could ever express!

Disclaimer

This book was written from my memories and from my perspective. Some names have been changed to protect the identity of all families involved. Also, some dates and times may be inaccurate in the beginning of the book, as I am going off of memories as a very small child, but I did try and stick as close to the way I remembered it as humanly possible.

Table of Contents

Foreword

She was a Chatty Cathy as a little one; I found it both trying and endearing. Lindsy was and is so full of life; she always has been. I value all my children, but Lindsy was different in that she was so full of joy and a love for life. She had such an innocence in the beginning of her life, only to be shattered by the enemy through his schemes and devices. You never had to wonder what was going on within her as a child because she was so open and honest about life and people, especially when younger. As she grew in age, the enemy found an inroad that caused her to sink into a place of fear and intimidation. He left her confused and destitute, angry and hurt, and hiding behind everything, a façade of smiles and laughter, concealing the deep wounds in her heart.

Her story is a miracle from the beginning because of the Lord's intervention. Every life has value, but the Lord fought for Lindsy! He had a plan and purpose for her from the beginning, and the enemy tried relentlessly to snuff her out. I am so grateful that the Lord spoke to me in the midst of pursuing an abortion; the Lord was letting me know, "I have a plan and a destiny for her." It is true for all my children, but Lindsy's life was on the line. Every child is of value, and the Father intervened to show me hers.

The cares of the world sometimes make us drunk, so drunk that on our own, we cannot see His ultimate plan for every life. The Lord will show up in the midst of all the confusion of your life and show you the way. Thank God! Her book is a book of hardship, but at the same time, it is a story of victory and hope, finding her way through it all with the help of Jehovah God! Her story is a story of restoration and rebuilding of a life, a marriage, and a family. There is always Hope in God!

Her story is a story of love, loss, and God's redemptive plan to make all things work together for our good! Faith is a fight, and the attack on her body, her life, and her family has always managed to turn her into the arms of the Father when things were at their worst. Lindsy is a fighter and a lover of God. Faith has a voice, and her voice is being heard in this book. Faith in the one true God! Surely, many will be able to relate to a woman who at one time felt so defeated, but God has shown her the way, given her grace and victory to continue hoping, believing, and receiving God's best for her life and family! My heart's desire is that everyone who reads this book may be able to relate to her experiences, and like Lindsy, they will find hope in the one true God who knows the beginning from the end, who has a plan and purpose for everyone and through and by His grace, we can all find our place of victory in Him!

The Lord is always the answer. I thank God every day that He makes a way where there seems to be no way, and He can take broken lives and make them whole and flourish. We serve an awesome God!

Pastor Debra Lee

It was November 15, 2000, when Dan, my husband, and I found ourselves at Freedom Life Church (then Freedom Tabernacle) in Kissimmee, Florida. We had just moved from Ohio because God had led us to. We were newly pregnant with our oldest daughter, though few people knew that, and we had a lot to learn. When Pastor Arthur Lee (Lindsy's stepfather) took the platform, we would have no way of knowing how much God would use him in our lives. He took one look at Dan and me and began to prophesy everything we were walking through. We knew that night that God had sent us to that church, and it was where we needed to grow.

Pastor Arthur (Poppy, as I called him) would become like a second father to me. Living across the country from all of my own extended family, the people of Freedom became our family. My children were extended grandchildren. To this day, that time in our lives is an example to me of what God intended when He talked about the church. God's desire isn't just to have four walls and padded pews but to truly become a family. Though time and miles have separated many of us as we've launched out into the things God has for us, that time, to me, is still so treasured and honored. Recently, I found myself in a situation, and it was Deb (Lindsy's mom) that I called for wise council. We will always be a family, and the reunion in heaven will be beautiful!

I met Lindsy and Robby in this season. I served on a praise and worship team with Robby for a time. Those were some services anointed by God. "The Storm" to this day is one of the songs that I binge-listen to whenever I'm going through something. I was in that "Celebration of Life" service when Robby first sang it publicly.

Lindsy reached out to me several years ago to help her get her story written and told. It was a project I gladly wanted to help her with. It became apparent to me early on; she needed to tell her story, and people needed to hear it. It is truly an honor to write this foreword.

Romans 8:28 (ESV) says, "And we know that for those who love God all things work together for good, for those who are called according to his purpose."

What Lindsy has walked through is challenging to read. It's tragic that these things happened. We live in a fallen world. However, God can use the "stuff" that we walk through, and if we allow Him, too, that "stuff" can be a beacon to others. It can show them how they can be an overcomer through Him. God is always faithful, even in the midst of the storm. I am so happy that she has found her voice. As you read these pages, know that just as God restored Lindsy's life, He can restore and redeem your story. I know, without a shadow of doubt, that Poppy would be so proud of her. That he is part of her heavenly cheering section (Hebrews 12:1).

Thank you for picking up this book. Let God speak to you as you read it. Life is too short, and we are a vapor. Find your voice, and blaze the trails God has for you!

With love and smiles,

Anna M. Aquino

Author & Guest Speaker

www.annamaquino.com

June 23, 2023

Chapter 1

FIRST ATTEMPT

"Before I formed you in the womb I knew you; Before you were born I sanctified you; I ordained you a prophet to the nations."

—Jeremiah 1:5 (NKJV)

Crawling out of bed and placing her feet one by one on the cold hardwood floor, she makes a mental note to buy a pair of slippers and leave them by the bed. *This floor is so cold*, she complains to herself. *Suck it up, Debra; you are going to have to rely on your parents from now on*, she realizes, at least until she gets back on her feet. Debra makes it a point to remember to thank her parents for being so kind to her during this very difficult time and helping her with the babies until she figures out all the details of her now very complicated life. God knows she has no one else to rely on. She glances over to the side of the bed where her two babies are sleeping. Toby, the oldest, is sleeping with her arms wrapped around her little sister, Brandi, in a protective manner. *With her blond hair lying across her face, she looks so angelic*, Debra thinks as she takes a mental picture to remember this moment. Brandi is resting peacefully in Toby's arms with her thumb in her mouth. Debra cannot recall a moment were they have looked this peaceful together. Sure, when they are alone, but not like this, not together. Debra takes a deep breath and decides it's time to get this dreaded day started.

She stands tall and stretches her arms to the ceiling, realizing just how bad her muscles are aching and her head is pounding, no doubt due to her endless crying till 4 a.m. this morning. She slowly walks to the bathroom and replays the events of the last few days in her head. How could this happen? How did she get here? She thought life was going to be so different and that she had found her happy ever after. It was young love, but now that she thinks about it, she realizes it was doomed from the start. What did she expect? He was with someone when he met her. She steps up to the mirror and looks at her reflection and starts to sob again. She sighs and then screams, will this nightmare ever end? She places her hand on her belly instinctively to protect her unborn child from the hurt raging inside her body like a fountain that never ends.

Grabbing a washcloth, she begins to wash her tear-stained face. Looking at her reflection, she sees the dark circles devouring her unique yellow eyes. Her baby fine hair, tangled from tossing and turning all night long. She grabs her toothbrush and her minty toothpaste and begins to scrub away the grime that has collected on her teeth. There she says to herself, *Starting to feel a little human again.* Starting the shower, she turns the knob to make it just the right temperature. *One degree below scolding, just how I like it,* she thinks to herself as she places her head under the shower head. Closing her eyes, she lets the hot water wash away all the sadness she feels saturating her very soul.

Once the hot water begins to run out, she steps out of the shower unto the floor, flinching the moment her toes touch the cold hardwood floors. She grabs a towel and wraps her hair like a turban and quietly walks to her closet. *What does one wear to the doctor's to end a human life?* she sadly wonders to herself. She decided to go with comfort. She grabs a white T-shirt and puts it over her head, and then she grabs her favorite pair of blue jeans and puts them on one leg at a time and carefully shimmies them into place, followed by pulling the zipper up and buttoning the top button. Exhausted, she looks in the mirror and thinks to herself, *Perfect.* She sits quietly back down on the bed and looks at her sleeping girls one more time before wiping away the new set of tears streaming down her face. She defeatedly stands up and pushes all her emotions as far down as she can before facing her family that awaits.

Now for the hard part; she heads through the archway leading to the kitchen, where she can hear the chattering of her family and the smell of breakfast in the air. Biscuits, ham, and red-eye gravy, her favorite. Genevieve, her mother, looks at her with annoyance and hands her a plate for her food.

"What, Mom? Why are you looking at me like that?"

"Shut up and eat your food," she says.

"I am serious; why are you looking at me like that?"

"You look awful; did you not get any sleep? Have you been crying all night? Debra, I told you he isn't worth it; you have to just let it go. Your dad and I can help you with the girls. You are not alone."

She rolls her eyes and says, "I know, Mom, but he was my husband, and we had a family. He wants a divorce; he wants to be with someone else. Do you know what that kind of rejection feels like? In a moment, I am a single mother of two, and my happy-ever-after is gone. I have nowhere to live. I have no money. I am trapped. I just want my life back. I want what he promised. I want my husband to hold me and tell me everything is going to be okay. I want my girls to have their daddy. They are so confused, asking for him all the time, and I don't know what to say or do. I just want this nightmare to end."

Her mother looks at her and says, "You have a home. Here. You have me and your dad. You are not alone; you will never be alone. We are family, and family sticks together."

My mother rolls her eyes, grabs her purse and a piece of toast, and heads to the car.

Her mother yells, "You didn't eat your breakfast."

Debra replied, "I can't stomach it today."

Sitting in her car with the keys in the ignition, she places her head on the steering wheel and begins to sob again. She thinks to herself, *How am I going to tell my mother that I am pregnant again? I just can't do it; no one can know; this must be done today.* She only lets the tears fall for a few minutes because she knows she has to be on time. So, she jerks her head up, adjusts the rearview mirror so she can fix her mascara, and then adjusts it back. She starts the car and begins to back out of the driveway of her mother and father's underground house they built in the middle of Kissimmee, Florida, just after a tornado destroyed the other one. She thinks to herself, *Can I do this? Can I start all over? Can I make this place feel like home?* With so many uncertainties, she drives to her destination on autopilot, flipping back and forth, battling within herself between what she wants and what she thinks must be done. As she pulls into the parking spot at this clinic, she feels a rush of urgency, but not knowing what it is, she continues on with her daily ritual of checking her makeup and hair in the rearview mirror. Once she is done, she puts the mirror back into place and steps out of the car and adjusts her clothes and begins to walk toward the clinic, emotions raging in every direction and fighting the uneasiness that has been flooding her soul for days.

The building looks much like it did the day before when Debra came for a preclinical experience, a desensitizing, if you will. She can still hear the sucking of the machine that they use to dispose of the fetus as they explained it. Chills running down her spine, she knows that something just isn't right, but she just pushes the feeling as far away as she can. She is doing what must be done, she tells herself. As she approaches, she sees the protesters just like the day before, but this time, she stops and reads their signs. The words of Jeremiah 29:11 (NKJV) flooding through her, "For I know the thoughts that I think toward you, says the Lord, thoughts of peace and not of evil, to give you a future and a hope," speaking to a part of her she doesn't even recognize. All the signs were so encouraging and shook her to the core, but more than that, the love on their faces penetrated her heart. One of the women walked up to Debra and told her, "You do not have to do this; you are not alone; God is with you." My mother politely thanked her and walked into the clinic, unable to shake this uneasiness seeping within her. Walking down the hall, full of fear and a world of disappointment, my mother is led into a cold and unwelcoming waiting room. The walls are painted sterile white, and the smell is bringing this morning's food up to the back of her throat. She was finally able to eat a piece of toast down between the uncontrollable sobs as she drove to the clinic and mentally prepared herself for this unbelievable task at hand. She has given herself the same speech for the last few days. "Debra, you can do it." "Debra, this is what has to be done." There were so many women waiting in the waiting room. As Debra looked around, she noticed some of the women were smiling and fine, like they had done this a million times, not a care in the world. Some of the others looked nervous, biting their nails with pale faces. Then there were the ones who were distraught like my mother, some even crying. Something just wasn't right; it was like something or someone was tugging on my mother's hearts strings for the last few days, and after the encounter outside with the woman and her sign, my mother could no longer shake this feeling. She thinks to herself, *What is taking the doctor so long?* She tries to steady her fears and calms her nerves, rehearsing in her mind the delicate words her friends and family have spoken into her life, how she was doing what had to be done, but still, the peace never comes.

Thoughts of my father, their tumultuous relationship, and their most recent decision to divorce resound in her soul. Being an unbeliever with no one to turn to, she cries out to herself. *How can I take much more? How much will I have to endure? The loss of myself, then my marriage, and now my unborn child.* She begins to imagine what the growing seed within her womb would look like, what will she call it, and then suddenly switches back to the words of her loved ones that she is indeed doing the right thing. This torment goes on for what seems like an eternity.

Then something changes in the atmosphere, and my mother, in her sin, in her fear, and in her darkest hour, finally gets an answer to the cries she has been crying for the past few days. Suddenly, a vision flashes before her eyes. It is a simple vision: she sees a line of cattle awaiting the slaughter. One by one, the cattle are killed. It was a gruesome and deadly scene, one she imagines will never be erased from her mind, a reminder for her, she knows, for years to come. Immediately, there was a quickening in my mother's spirit, a knowing that God, whoever He was, was showing her that these cows were really pregnant women slaughtering their babies. My mother jumps up and gathers her belongings; she is so frazzled that she struggles with her things for a few seconds before she finally has all her stuff together, all the while chanting to herself, *I am so sorry baby, I didn't know*. She has a newfound peace that comes from knowing. Just as she heads for the door, the doctor enters the room. She thinks to herself, *Thank God you took so long.*

He looks at her with confusion and asks, "Mrs. Taylor, is everything okay?"

My mother looks at him with confidence in her eyes, a confidence she had recently lost in the past few years due to a marriage of lies and deceit, and says, "Everything is great. I was just leaving."

The doctor interrupts her and says, "Leaving? Why? Can we talk about this first?"

"No! I am leaving. I made a mistake; there is nothing you can say to change my mind."

The doctor puts his head down in defeat and clears a path

for my mother to walk through. Broken yet strengthened, my mother grabs her things and heads off down the hall with a newfound purpose in her heart.

As she sits in the car and puts her seatbelt across her lap, she replays the experiences that she just had with God. She is still shaking and feeling this overwhelming peace that only comes from the Father. Placing her keys into the ignition, she starts the car and heads back to her mother and father's, replaying the last few years in her mind. As she drives on autopilot, she thinks, *My marriage wasn't all bad.* A memory of Tony floods her thoughts. It was a cold rainy day in Germany in their little cottage on base. My mother and father were sitting at home, bored with nothing to do. My mom was homesick for her family and homeland, feeling very depressed when my father walked into the room with two tampons stuck up his nose. He says, "Hey, Debra, look." Debbie swings around and sees her silly husband and his crude behavior and laughs uncontrollably. She smiles and even lets out a laugh at the memory. Tony had a way about him that could make her laugh. Not just a simple laugh but a deep belly laugh. He was beautiful and, at times, made her feel like she was the only person standing in a room. That is the part she is going to miss the most, their ability to have fun together and laugh. Then suddenly, she is saddened again at his betrayals; if only he could have stayed faithful. She always knew he had a selfish side but never had a problem overlooking it until he was unfaithful. The one thing she could not fault him on was his love for Toby and Brandi. He loved to spend time with them and play with them. He loved to take them for walks and to the park. He was such a good daddy when he wasn't otherwise preoccupied with certain addictions. She is so very hopeful that even though their marriage is over and that he has moved on, he will not abandon the children that they have made together. Her heart aches for her babies. Babies that are innocent and did not ask for any of this. She begins to doubt that she can shield them from the heartache of the years ahead, for what she knows is in store. All at once, this feeling of warm, thick honey slowly makes its way over her body from her head to her feet, and the peace she felt at the doctor's office floods her again.

Arriving at the house, her father, Bernard, was shucking oysters with family all around.

Her mother walks up to her and says, "So, you okay?"

Debra looks at her mother and says, "I will be."

Relief floods Jenny's face as she hugs her mom and says, "Everything is going to be just fine."

They walked toward the rest of the family, and Debra

thought to herself, *This is what family is all about*. For the first time in days, everything was so clear. She didn't know how, but she just knew everything was going to be okay! She looks at her mother and says, "Mom, I am pregnant."

This was the day that my mother chose life; she chose me by the grace and calling of God. The devil fought hard to take me out before I even got started. But God, in His infinite wisdom and His ability to see the end, decided to fight for my life and give me a chance to do what I was called to do. I will be forever grateful that my mother heeded God's voice and gave me the opportunity to live out my destiny.

My mother told me this story when I was in the fifth grade. I was in speech class and had to do a speech about myself. At first, it was so shocking to hear that my mother was going to have an abortion. I thought I was almost not here. I wasn't angry with my mother. I knew she was going through hell and back. I can only imagine what it's like to have your world flipped upside down and everything changing, especially with children involved. To tell you the truth, I was in awe of my mother, to know where she came from to where she is now. I only hope I could be so strong. Little did I know my trails had only begun in life and that my strength and perseverance would be tested as well. And so, the journey begins. Join me as I tell the tale of the journey through my perspective, both good and bad, that led me to the one thing the devil tried so hard to destroy and to silence, my voice!

Chapter 2

2017: PRESENT DAY

"Trust in the Lord with all your heart, And lean not on your own understanding; In all your ways acknowledge Him, And He shall direct your paths."

—Proverbs 3:5–6 (NKJV)

There has always been a small part of me that just didn't seem complete. A part of me that didn't feel and wasn't awakened, a piece that died, how I just don't know. Was it this one event that started in the beginning while I was just a seed, or was it the combination of many events that shattered my soul into a million pieces and turned me into the empty shell that I had become? A person so bound by fear and a person without a voice.

The one thing I have learned on this journey is that hate, bitterness, unforgiveness, jealousy, fear, and anger are a poison that will kill you slowly without you even knowing it. I have tried many paths and avenues to fill the void that only God can fill. I have worn the scarlet letter with shame more than once in an attempt to be released from a marriage I thought wasn't for me. I have contemplated suicide multiple times. I have run to drugs and alcohol to numb the pain, and I have put myself through school and worked myself till all resources from my body were depleted and my body started to attack itself. But hear me now, none, and I mean none, of the above things worked. They only further silenced my voice and bound my soul in chains.

There is a bigger picture here, a great divide; heaven and hell are contending for your very soul. Satan and his legions will stop at nothing to snuff you out and shut down your voice, knowing it is the one thing that can set you free and set the captives free around you. The longer you stay silent, the longer God's people suffer. There is freedom that shakes the universe when you release the sound of your voice and the words of your testimony. I have finally come to the place where I am able to see the bigger picture through a series of events that have taken place starting at the time of obedience in August 2016.

The Lord had been gently tugging on Robby and me to move to Tennessee for several years with no success. We had hit an all-time low. Robby bought a boat, and I was in full-fledged career mode. He decided he would just spend his time fishing and let go of ministry. I was so independent and broken I convinced myself I was not what Robby needed and that I was the very reason he could not reach his purpose; I was his Delilah; I quenched his anointing, and he deserved better. I had nothing but brokenness to offer him, and I had broken him too many times. So, while he was fishing, I was planning my divorce and was going to try the grass on the dark side of the tracks; after all, isn't that where I truly belonged? But, then God! Little did we know God had us right where He wanted us. Once Robby said, "I know God told us to go, but I have decided to stay right where I am at," that's the moment God withdrew to show us just how dark it can get. It didn't take long for us to realize we messed up big time.

So, what did we do? We turned to one another and turned to God. We repented and said, "Yes, Lord." That was just the beginning of a long journey that we now find ourselves on. A journey of healing. A journey of forgiveness. A journey to a new us. The us He always intended for us to be.

It wasn't until we moved to Tennessee that I realized this wasn't going to be easy. I did not know how deep the wounds for either of us went, but I did know we both said yes and made a vow to give it all we had. The problem lies in the fact that it didn't matter our location on a map if we didn't deal with the deep-rooted issues that brought us to the state we were in. I did not know just how broken and shattered my soul was. I was just focused on the pain I felt somedays and the numbness I felt other days. I was so focused on myself, what I was denied, what happened to me, what I didn't get, or how unfair life was. I failed to see the bigger picture that surrounded me. There are people dying, broken, and bound by chains, and this was the beginning of the journey God was taking me on to heal me and turn my focus onto this lost and dying world.

Throughout this story, I will be jumping back and forth in time to try and paint a picture of my life, how I was silenced, and the struggles I endured that further bound me. Some of these struggles are due to bad decisions I have made, and others are due to other people's bad decisions.

My story is not all bad. I will also tell of some of the pearls I received along the way that were precious little gifts from God to help me hold on. I am grateful for the good and the bad times in my life. They have taught me so much. Some parts of my life are so shameful they were merely impossible to address in writing, but I know someone needs to hear it. I only hope that my story will reach at least one person and help them to lose their chains and give them total freedom so they can reach many and God's people will no longer be bound by their past.

I have by no means arrived. I am still a work in progress, and I am sure it will take years for me to even scratch the surface. All I know is as I write, even the shameful things are broken, and I feel lighter. God has me right where He wants me. I refuse to be silent anymore. I will stand by my husband, and we will answer the call of the Father together as God has intended. Our focus will no longer be on us, but our shift will be to the captives lost and bound by fear and shame, to show them the way, the truth, and the light! There is a hope: His name is Jesus.

Chapter 3

1983: MY FIRST MEMORY

"This is My commandment, that you love one another as I have loved you."

—John 15:12 (NKJV)

The light was shining through the window above my dresser into my eyes as I opened them, trying to avoid the shock of the morning from slapping me in the face. I remember this sense of peace that only a little girl in a home full of love could feel. I looked across the room to the bed adjacent to mine, and there she was, my sissy Brandi! The thought still makes me smile today.

My room was like any other three-year-old's room. I had toys thrown about from the day before playing hard with my sisters. We often played so hard, leaving our toys carelessly wherever they fell. Like any three-year-old on a mission for mystery and imagination with the attention of a squirrel, going from one room to another, forgetting what I was just playing and landing a new idea and role to play. I shared a room with my sister, Brandi; she was five and so much wiser than my three years of experience on this earth. We had two beds on opposite sides of the wall, separated by a dresser. My room was my favorite place in the house due to my toys and my great imagination that my room was my castle and I was a princess.

As I sat up in my bed and looked over at my sister sleeping so soundly with her thumb in her mouth, I became very anxious. *What will I do until she wakes up? She is my only friend and my most bestest friend in the whole wide world*, I thought to myself. I slowly creeped out of bed and tried to quietly walk over to hers. As I tripped over a toy lying on the floor and landed on her bed, I scrunched my eyes really tight in hopes of making myself disappear. I was so afraid she would be mad, even though I rarely remember my sister Brandi ever being unkind to me. I slowly peeked through one eye to see what my calamity had caused, only to see her looking at me with her thumb in her mouth and her smiling around it. I knew everything was going to be okay after that. She slowly sat up and scooted over to make a place for me beside her for me to play while we waited for Toby to wake up. This was our morning routine. She sat in bed quietly beside me while I played with my dolls. I looked over at her, and I said, "Brandi, I am hungry," in a whinny voice.

She said, "You will have to wait till Toby wakes up to eat," with a sarcastic look on her face as her eyes rolled to the back of her head. I continued to play as I knew better than to wake my big sister up. She could be grumpy in the mornings if you woke her up too soon. It was always better to wait for her to come into our room than to go into hers. I heard Mom yelling at Toby one time that she had a lot of responsibility and needed to make sure what needed to be done was done. I think that's why Toby can be grumpy sometimes. Today is a little different because Pooh Bear usually watches while my mother is at work, but today, she had an emergency, so it's just me, Brandi, and Toby. Toby is very good to us, and sometimes she even plays with us when she isn't too busy.

My sister Toby slept in the room across the hall with my mother. She is taking care of us today while my mommy is at work. She is really big; she is eight years old. She helps a lot with the cooking and cleaning because Mommy has to work. She also makes sure we do the right things while Mommy is at work, and sometimes she even takes us to the grocery store in my red wagon to get groceries. I love riding in the red wagon to the store with my sisters; it is such a fun adventure even though going back home, I have to walk sometimes because there is no room in the wagon. I don't think my sister likes it too much; she sometimes gets annoyed and yells when I am not doing the right things or when I am in Lindsy's world chasing bugs instead of looking out for cars. She gets to buy the groceries with these really cool stamps. I think they are very pretty. But, for some reason, my mother doesn't like them very much. That is why she makes Toby take us in the red wagon. Toby always gets my favorite bean and bacon soup and Lay's potato chips.

Once we get home, we usually take the Lay's chips and mustard and eat on the back steps and play with Tar-Baby, my kitty, because Toby doesn't like us to make a mess in the house. Tar-Baby is black and white and loves to be petted. Brandi and I sit out back and eat our chips and play with Tar-Baby until we are done. This is pretty much our routine.

Today, however, we didn't go shopping; that wasn't going to be for a few more days. So, Brandi and I decided to play "Save the Princess." I was on my bed, and she was on hers, and the space between our beds was shark-infested waters. So we opened the third drawer down to the dresser and decided I would walk across to her bed to safety. It wasn't until I got halfway across that I realized I was in big trouble. I froze in fear as the dresser teetered and eventually landed on me with my back to the floor. I felt instant pain; I couldn't breathe. My sister Brandi was screaming hysterically for Toby to help as she tried to lift it unsuccessfully off me. At that moment, Toby runs through the door, fear and anger all over her face. She demanded for Brandi to grab one side as she grabbed the other. She told Brandi, "At the count of three, push up as hard as you can." Toby counted one, two, three, and instantly, I could breathe again, but the dresser drawers fell out onto me. I was so scared. Toby snatched me up and checked my body for injuries. She held me and told me everything was going to be okay, followed by, "What were you thinking?" She was relieved but irritated all at the same time. Brandi walked around and hugged me from the opposite side. I was now a Toby and Brandi sandwich. At that very moment, I, three years old, in my mother's duplex, felt the safest and most loved I had ever felt. I knew that my sisters loved me and would take care of me no matter what.

Later on that evening, around four o'clock, my tummy started rumbling and burning. I leaned over to my sister Brandi and whispered, "Are you hungry?"

Brandi said, "Yes. Shhh, it's because we forgot to eat lunch today." Sometimes, this would happen when we were playing too hard or when Toby didn't feel like cooking. So, I walked into the living room, where Toby was folding laundry and watching the end of her soap show. I climbed onto the couch and put my thumb into my mouth until the commercial came on so I didn't make her mad. Once the commercial came on, I, twirling my hair in my fingers, slurped up the slobber around my thumb and said, "Toby, I am hungry; do we have anything to eat?"

Toby puts the half-folded sheet down and says, "Yes, but we are going to walk to Gammy's today because I don't feel like cooking. She cooks better, and Mom is running late."

"But I don't feel like walking that far," I complained.

"Well, I tried to call, but there was no answer."

"What about Pooh Bear?" I whined. That's our babysitter who lives next door.

"She is not home today; she had an emergency," Toby replied. "Guess what tomorrow is," said Toby, trying to distract me.

I shrugged my shoulders, not knowing.

"Friday!" said Brandi.

I sat back and thought for a minute, and a smile crept up on my face, "Yes! McDonald's." Every other Friday was Mommy's payday, and she always took us for a Happy

Meal. Then, suddenly, I began to frown. I looked at Toby with my big blue eyes into her beautiful green eyes with tears misting up; I said, "So we have to wait until tomorrow to eat?"

Toby's shoulders shrank as if the weight of the world landed on them, and she put her head down and said, "No, silly, we are going to go to Gammy's. I just don't feel like cooking right now."

Toby sat up straight and said, "Girls, get your shoes on; we are going to walk to Gammy and Gampy's now." I slap my little hands together with an excitement that can't be contained. Princess Lindsy gets to go to Gammy's castle today. Oh boy, it feels like Christmas! My Gammy has a true-life castle. My Gampy built it when a tornado tore their old house down to the ground. It is a house built in a mountain. It has a stone wall all the way across the front with a courtyard in the middle with a cellar and a garage workshop for Gampy. The front door was a massive, arched wooden door that was too hard for me to open. Once you walk through the first wooden door, it's a small hall to another matching arched wooden door; in that hallway, on the wall is hanging a newspaper article with my sister Toby's pictures holding her teddy bear looking through the scraps of her old room that the tornado tore down. My sister remembers the tornado, but I do not. My mommy says that cinder blocks landed in my crib just as she grabbed me out of it. She said I almost died, but I do not remember it. My mom said that after that, Gampy said he was going to build something that could not ever be destroyed again, and that's how he came about building the castle.

My Gammy and my Gampy are my favorite people in the whole world. They always make me really good food and give me hugs and make sure I am clean. My favorite part about going to Gammy's house is waking up to the adults talking in the kitchen and walking through the arches to my Gammy asking me what I want for breakfast. So, when Toby announced we were walking to my Gammy's, you can clearly see why I would be so excited. I jumped up and ran about the house, looking for my favorite jelly shoes. They were purple. After what seemed to be a lifetime, I walked over to Toby and whined, "Toby, I can't find my shoes."

She looked down at me sternly and stated, "Did you look in your closet?"

I shook my head yes.

She looked up and yelled at Brandi, "Help Lindsy find her shoes."

Brandi rolled her eyes and flicked my arm, saying, "You probably didn't even look, did you?"

I shook my head in protest and said, "Yes, I did."

Finally, Toby said, "Forget it; we are going anyway; we have to go before it gets dark." She made sure the lights were off and then headed for the road with both of us close behind. We walked on the main road only for a few minutes before we cut through the backfield that eventually led to Gammy's.

"Toby, are we almost there?" I complained as the sun started to set. "It's getting dark, and I am still so very hungry."

Toby grabbed my hand tightly and said in a stern voice, "I know, Lindsy. We are almost there."

I stopped in pain as a sticker penetrated my foot; Brandi offered me her body to lean on as Toby pulled the sticker out. "The sun is almost gone," I said as we walked up to the huge wooden door to my Gammy's.

Toby said nothing; I think she is irritated with me again.

We walk into Gammy's; she does not seem very happy. She looks at Toby and says, "How did you get here?"

Toby answered, "We walked."

She grabbed me in her arms and said, "You made these babies walk all the way here. What were you thinking? Someone could have been hurt or killed."

Toby looked at Gammy with tears in her eyes; she said, "The phone was not working, and Mom is running late. Pooh Bear had an emergency, and I didn't have much to cook. Brandi and Lindsy were starving; I didn't know what else to do."

Gammy said, "Okay, okay. You guys are here now, and you are safe. Let's get you cleaned up and fed." Gammy set me on the kitchen table and gave me a good looking at. She found a bubble on the bottom of my foot. She called it a blister. She put me in her giant bathtub with Brandi and filled it up with bubbles while she made supper. I felt like a real-life princess.

Toby came into the bathroom with her hair wet and combed and said, "Okay, you guys, it's time to eat. Time to get out and get dressed." Toby dried me off and helped me with my clothes and combed my hair. As we walked into the kitchen, I stopped to look at the wall of candles my Gammy had collected over the years. I found my favorite one of the deer at the waterfall and petted the deer on the head, then headed toward the wonderful smell coming from the kitchen. I sat in my spot at the table as Gammy placed bean and bacon soup with some crackers in front of me. *Heaven*, I said to myself as I grabbed my spoon and looked around the table. Gammy, Gampy, Toby, and Brandi, and bean and bacon soup; life just can't get any better than this.

We sat and ate as Gammy talked to us about what we did today. I told her about how the dresser almost killed me, but my sisters saved my life. Her mouth dropped open, and she told me all the reasons why that was not a good idea. I hung my head in shame as she told me about safety and why we should not have walked that far without an adult. Then she said she was so glad we were there and that we were safe. She said, "Your mother is going to be so worried looking for you. Maybe she will let you spend the night tonight, and when she gets off work tomorrow, she can take you to McDonald's. We all started jumping up and down in excitement because we loved staying at Gammy's house.

My mother showed up a few minutes later; she was not happy; her face was all scrunched up and red as she took Toby to the side. Toby was crying. I don't know why everyone is so upset, but they are. My mom drops to her knee and hugs Toby. Toby isn't really hugging my mommy back; her arms are straight, and she looks mad with her face all scrunched up. Toby comes and sits by me and says, "It's just not fair. I make sure you get fed, and I am the one who gets in trouble." I lean my head on Toby, and I am thankful that she brought me here for food even if the grown-ups are mad.

My mother finally agrees to allow us to spend the night with Gammy. She comes into the living room, gives us all hugs and kisses, and says, "I will pick you up tomorrow when I get off work for our special dinner." My mommy starts to walk to the door when I run after her for one more hug. She leans over, squeezes me tight, and tells me she loves me, and then I run back into the living room with my sisters and Gampy. Gampy was lying on his beanbag playing with Toby and Brandi; I jumped in with a squeal and started defending my sisters.

Later on that night, it was time to go to bed. My Gammy made us a huge pile on the floor with pillows and fluffy blankets. We all got into place. Toby is on the outside, in a protective position, then Brandi lies down with her thumb in her mouth, and I take the last spot closest to the wall. I put my thumb in my mouth and start twirling my hair with my other hand. My Gampy is at the base of us on his beanbag watching *Jeopardy*; it's his favorite. He always seems to get all the questions right. As I start to drift asleep,

I think about how lucky I am. I have all my sisters. I have a mommy who works so hard that I get McDonald's every other week on Friday. I have a Gammy and a Gampy with a real-life princess castle. And when I fall asleep at night, I have everything I could possibly need. My family.

This is the first memory I can remember. I was three, and we were a struggling family. My mother worked hard, and my sister did more than an eight-year-old should have to, but we were a functioning family. I did not realize the severity of my situation then because I felt so loved and so taken care of. I knew as long as my mom, Toby, Brandi, or Gammy and Gampy were there, I was going to be okay. It was all I knew, and I was grateful for everything I had.

As I walked through this memory, I realized on this day that family is everything. I learned that no matter how poor, how busy, or how hard things may be, as long as you have each other, you have all you need. This was still only the beginning of what was in store. These lessons I was learning as a baby were the stepping stone to the harder lessons to come. God was showing me through my very young years how no matter what the situation, He is always in control, and He will take care of me always.

Little did I know somewhere in the near future, my life was going to change forever for the better. He was going to give me and my family a gift that would write a new story, a story of redemption in the midst of rejection. Some of us would take this gift with joy, some of us not so much. But this is my story, so I will tell you how it changed me forever. These were going to be the years of learning a new way of life.

"But the mercy of the Lord is from everlasting to everlasting On those who fear Him, And His righteousness to children's children" (Psalm 103:17, NKJV).

Chapter 4

PRESENT DAY: FAMILY

"The thief does not come except to steal, and to kill, and to destroy. I have come that they may have life, and that they may have it more abundantly."

—**John 10:10 (NKJV)**

I have two pictures painted in my mind, one from conception and the other from my first memories as a child. When I think of these two memories, I can see the works of God from the beginning. What Satan meant to destroy from the beginning, God intended to redeem. What was meant as the ultimate rejection and murder of my soul through abortion and the unwanted atmosphere of the womb due to pain and divorce, God turned it around by crying out for my soul Himself. It was not my time to die. I still had so much to do and so much to say! He knew my potential long before anyone else did.

As I dissected my very first memory, I began to see this beautiful picture He was painting for me. A picture of family, despite the brokenness and the trials and poorness of it all. In fact, He began to show me just how rich we really were because we had each other, and we would have done anything for one another. It didn't matter that my father abandoned us and that I so desperately wanted a father in my life. What really mattered was that in the very heartbeat of my world, I had people surrounding me who loved me and would have done anything for me that was within their power.

God was weaving a masterpiece, my life, with His ultimate plan in mind.

Knowing there would be more that I would have to endure and leaving room for my mistakes. I now know He, my heavenly Father, never left me. He was with me all the time. He wept when I wept; He wanted justice when wrongs were done and ached for me to let all of it go and run to Him, so my life could truly begin. So, He patiently waited until I was ready. Ready to forgive Him, ready to forgive myself, and ready to forgive the ones who broke me.

What happens next will change the course of my life dramatically for the better. It was everything we needed, and it was right on time. God is so good.

Chapter 5

1985: WHEN WE MET

"Sing to God, sing praises to His name; Extol Him who rides on the clouds, By His name Yah, And rejoice before Him. A father to the fatherless, a defender of widows, Is God in His holy habitation. God sets the solitary in families; He brings out those who are bound into prosperity; But the rebellious dwell in a dry land."

—Psalm 68:4–6 (NKJV)

I run to my closet and scrunch down in a panic; my heart is beating out of my chest as I hear my mother yell through the door to find my shoes before we are late for church. My current state has me too flustered to even think straight. I stop and calm my nerves by breathing in and out real slow. I straighten my braids with my hands and try to think where I threw them last. It is useless; I will never find them, and we are going to be late. So, I stand up and quietly wade through the mess. I trip on my book bag and land slap dab on top of the very thing I have been desperately trying to find. I grab the right one first and put it on as quickly as I can, and then I grab the left and do the same. I am so excited; I get to go to our new church and meet new friends. I picked out my favorite dress today, the blue one with strips. *It's perfect; everyone will love it,* I think to myself. "Mom," I yell, running into the living room, "I found my shoes." Relieved, she let out a sigh and called for everyone to get in the car.

Toby yells, "I call front seat," as she heads to the car. I know better than to even fight for that spot; I am too little, and no one ever lets me sit up front. Toby takes her place in the front seat with a smile of pleasure on her face. Brandi crosses her arms over one another in anger. Toby demands her to get into the car and quit being such a baby.

"I am not a baby," Brandi protests. "It's just not fair you always sit up front," she says.

Toby replies, "It is because I am the oldest; get over it."

Brandi jumps into the back seat and looks out the window in deep thought. I know better than to disturb her. I crawl into my spot and put my thumb into my mouth and twirl my thin, dirty blond hair in my fingers. I drift in thought about what today may be like. Oh no! What if they don't like me? What if they are mean? The thought fades away quickly, and I begin to think about what games we might play and what snacks we might have. My mom puts the car in gear and backs out of the driveway. "All right, here we go," she proclaims. My belly flutters for the second time today, but this time in anticipation of the unknown.

Pulling into the parking spot, I get a good look of the church building; it is a simple white building with a steeple. It wasn't as large and extravagant as I envisioned it would be. It was small and average, but something about it was so inviting. I looked at the other families getting out of their cars, looking to see if there were any kids my age. My heart started picking up a beat when I saw a family with several kids getting out of the van, and some did, in fact, look to be my age.

Maybe they will be my friends, I thought. I slowly climbed out of the car and straightened my dress and my braids in hopes of looking presentable. My new church, whatever that means. My mom sat me down and told me we would start going to church; she said there would be other kids there my age. Well, that's all it took. I love making friends, and I love getting together and playing games and having snacks. My mother grabbed me by the hand and said, "You ready?"

I took a deep breath and said, "Yep, let's go."

We headed into the church through the front doors. There were some really nice people who handed my mom a piece of paper, and the nice man patted me on the head and smiled at me. I just returned the smile with the biggest, cheesiest smile I could. My mother leads us through the next set of doors; as we walk through, I see a really big room with a stage and lots and lots of chairs. My eyes got big; there were so many people I am suddenly feeling nervous. I noticed that as we walked through the doors, my sisters and I got incredibly closer to my mom, like she was shielding us from the unknown. My mom, trying to greet the people with hugs, gently freed her arms from our grasp and leaned in to hug the people as they approached. Finally, my mother led us to a set of chairs and said, "Okay, everyone, pick a seat." I chose the one closest to my mother. I suddenly was more scared than excited. My mother sat down and gave me a kiss on my head. She leaned down and whispered to us that everything was fine and this was going to be fun, she promised.

The next thing I know, the music starts playing. It is real live music. Mom leans over to me and says, "That is Pastor Janice." I thought to myself, *That is the most beautiful woman I have ever seen*; her hair was blond and fixed perfectly, not a hair out of place. She was small-framed and had tiny features on her face. Her makeup was painted perfectly on. She had a voice of an angel. I was mesmerized until the very last song. Partly because of her beauty but also partly because of the feeling I was feeling as they were singing their song. I have heard many songs, but never had a song made me feel like this; it was calming and peaceful, almost warming. When Pastor Janice was done with the last song, Pastor Gary walked up to the stage to make announcements. He dismissed the children for children's church, and my mom looked at me with anticipation. I shook my head no; "I want to stay with you," I whined.

She said, "Lindsy, you said you wanted to go."

"I know what I said, but I don't want to now."

She said, "What if Brandi goes with you?"

Now we were both looking at her, shaking our heads no. She pleaded quietly for a few seconds before we finally gave in and stood up to go. Relieved, she stood to lead the way. That's the time a nice lady appeared and said she would show us the way. We reluctantly left our mom and headed toward the children's church building, which was beside the building we were in. As we made it outside, my apprehension eased a little. As we got closer to the children's church building, I could hear the children's laughter. I could hear another song, but this time, it was in a special voice, and the other children were begging for whoever to sing it again. My belly started to turn with excitement as I walked through the doors. I looked in the direction of the children begging for the puppet to sing it again; it was then I realized what was going on. There was a stage with curtains up. You could not see any people, just the puppets sitting on the skirt of the stage. I guess there were grown-ups behind the curtains controlling the puppets even though I could not see them with my eyes. I thought to myself, *This is amazing and perfect, and I get to come every week.*

The puppet is sitting there waiting for all the kids to grab their seats and settle in. He introduced himself as Leroy, and all the children said, "Hi, Leroy," all together as if this was something they do often. The children were begging him to sing a song. "All right, all right, all right," Leroy protested. "You want to sing a song; let's sing a song." Leroy started off singing a song that the children knew well; they all sang along as he started off with, "All God's children love living, living, all God's children love wander bread." The instant he said "wander bread," all the kids protested loudly, "That's not how it goes," and

Leroy would stop and look around and say, "Oh, I must have forgotten," and start all over again messing up from time to time and having to start all over again. Until he finally did the whole song without messing up. The song went like this, "All God's children love living, living; all God's children love living bread; all God's children love living, living; all God's children love living bread; so throw up your hands and fall on your face; the Holy Ghost is gonna shake this place." All the kids were captivated by Leroy, the song, the mess up, and having to redo the song. I thought, *I wonder what the person with the puppet looks like*. Leroy finally finishes his act and excuses himself and quietly goes back behind the stage. The whole room is silent in anticipation of what is coming next.

Then there he was, the man behind the puppet erupts from behind the stage. He looks to be young; he has dark brown hair that waves to the side. He is super skinny and not too tall. His eyes are a unique yellow, but more than that, there is a light in his eyes I have never seen before. They are glowing, and there is so much kindness in his face. Love and happiness radiate off him as he smiles at me from around the corner. There is something safe and calming about his presence. I look around and see the other kids are drawn to him too. Their faces are locked onto his, and there is total engagement. It's like he is the only person in the room. *I don't ever want to go home*, I think to myself. I can't wait to tell my mom about this. When he spoke, you had to listen because you never knew what was coming out of his mouth. You could tell he loved children and loved what he did because he really saw us, not like the other grown-ups. He would speak and listen to our replies. He never seemed angry or overwhelmed by our rambunctiousness. He wasn't like any other grown-up I had ever seen or known before. We played games and ate yummy snacks. As the morning started coming to a close, I began to be sad. I didn't want it to be over. But I knew there would always be next week. They talked a lot about this man named Jesus, a man I don't know. They talk about this man as being alive, but I think He is dead. Arthur keeps saying that He died but rose again. He says that Jesus is alive and will live in you if you ask Him. I am not sure I want some man living in me, but maybe one day I might change my mind. Arthur prays for all the kids, and some of them fall. *I do not want to be prayed for if I have to fall*, I think to myself. I think Arthur knew my apprehension because he did not pressure me at all; he just let me watch and would occasionally smile at me. He dismissed the service, and I bolted toward my mother. "Mom, Mom, they had a puppet show and snacks and played games and told me about a man named Jesus," I told her as she got closer to me.

My mother said, "Shhh, slow down, baby; I don't understand what you are saying; you are talking too fast." My big sister came up and acted as my translator as I had a horrible speech problem, and she was really the only one who understood me. My mom grabbed my hand and smiled, pleased that we had a good time, and headed back to the car we arrived in.

All the way home, Brandi and I told my mother about our time in children's church. My mother just listened with a smile on her face. Something is different about my mother lately; she smiles more. "I am so glad you have fun," she says as she pulls into the driveway of our duplex. I jumped out and headed toward Tar-Baby. I picked her up and put her on my lap as I sat on the ground. "Get off the ground with your dress on; go inside and change first," my mother protests. I put Tar-Baby back on the ground and head into the house, wiping my dress off with my hands. As I take my dress off and change into my play clothes, I think about what the man at church said. I don't understand it all, but I know it is significant, and one day, it is going to mean something special. I lie in my bed with my toys and think about Leroy and the song he sang. I can't remember all of it, but I am singing the beginning part, "All God's children love living, living; all God's children love living bread," in my head on repeat as I wait for supper to be ready. *Arthur*, I said to myself. What a great person, so much fun and full of light. Little did I know he was going to be a huge part of my life in every way possible.

Chapter 6

PRESENT DAY: JUST WHAT WE NEEDED

"Thus says the Lord of hosts: 'Execute true justice,
Show mercy and compassion Everyone to his brother. Do
not oppress the widow or the fatherless, The alien or the
poor. Let none of you plan evil in his heart Against his
brother."

—Zechariah 7:9–10 (NKJV)

Arthur Jackson Lee was a breath of fresh air and right on time. Our family had been striving to survive and missing an essential piece: a father. I love to think that God loved us so much and searched the earth for the perfect father figure to pick up the pieces and show us the love of our heavenly Father, and He found us Arthur; what a gift.

This was the time in my life when I felt things began to make sense and be in order. Through a series of events, Arthur and my mother fell deeply in love and got married. Arthur, despite my mother's heavy load, took us all in as his own and loved us through the challenges that came with three instant daughters who were broken and unsure about life.

He had a lot of rules, made a lot of changes, and was met with a lot of resistance. He never missed a beat. He just took it, stood his ground, and loved us anyway. He ran a tight ship. I loved him from the start; he was just what my soul needed. Someone who loved away my pain. I will always be grateful to him for that.

Sometimes in life, God gives us gifts, something or someone special to guide us through and to either help show us the way or just make life better. That is what Arthur was for me. I am not sure how long after this memory he married my mother, but he did. He became my father. I was lacking a lot. I was lacking the knowledge of God, I was lacking a spiritual father, and I was lacking the love of a natural father. Then, one day, in God's boundless mercy, He smiled down on me and said, "I will give her just what she needs." From the moment Arthur entered my life until the moment he exited his natural body and entered heaven, he was everything I needed and even more. My life was forever changed by this man. He taught me so much. How to love and be loved. How to have fun. How to work hard. How to be someone you are proud of. He was so patient and gentle and kind. He treated my mother like gold. He came in and helped put all the pieces of our broken family back together again. He was met with much resistance from my sister Toby, who felt like he was taking her place even though her place was a heavy burden she shouldn't have to bear. It didn't matter; none of it mattered to him; he loved us anyway.

I often think to myself, *What kind of man takes on a woman with three kids with so much resistance and continues to plow forward and try to show them in the midst of their rejection and brokenness what love is? Real love.* Over the years, I got to know him better than most, and he was real. He was who he said he was inside and out. What you saw in public was what he was in private. A lover of Jesus and a man of his word. Sometimes, I like to think he saved the best parts of himself for us. We got to see the best of him. But he had a way of making everyone feel like that. To know him was an absolute pleasure, a treasure. I thank God every day for letting him be in our lives even if it was for just a little while.

"Learn to do good; Seek justice, Rebuke the oppressor; Defend the fatherless, Plead for the widow" (Isaiah 1:17, NKJV).

Chapter 7

1986: THE DAY I ASKED JESUS INTO MY HEART

"But Jesus said, 'Let the little children come to Me, and do not forbid them; for of such is the kingdom of heaven.'"

—**Matthew 19:14 (NKJV)**

For fear of running late for church, I grabbed the clothes my mother had picked out for me the night before. I sighed as I examined the dress she chose. It was green with ruffles and my sister's favorite. She recently grew out of the dress, and so now I have adopted the hideous thing. I am six years old and the smallest in my family, so that means I very rarely get my own new dress. I get most of my sister's clothes she grows out of, and even some of them she got from my oldest sister Toby. Now, normally, this didn't bother me because I always loved my sister's clothes and couldn't wait for them to be mine. However, today, at this moment, that is not the case. I put the dress on and walk

65

toward my door. I am so sleepy; my hair is matted and tangled. I am more grumpy than usual.

When I walk through my bedroom door, my house is alive and moving. My sisters are already at the table eating their cereal. Toby looks particularly grumpy this morning. I make a mental note to leave her alone. I walk over to the place my mother set for me and sit down with a frown on my face. No one seems to notice my mood. I grab the box of Lucky Charms and pour it into the bowl, followed by some milk. Lucky Charms is my favorite cereal to eat in the mornings. As I eat my cereal, I feel my mood shift. I find food has this effect on me; it always seems to lighten my mood. I get up from the table and search for my mother, who always fixes my hair.

She is a little flustered this morning; I note as I enter her bathroom. She has the curling iron in her hair as she notices me entering the room. "Lindsy," my mother says with a stern, motherly voice, "you need to brush your hair."

"I can't find the brush, Mommy, and you need to fix my hair; I can't do it."

"I don't have time right now," she says. "I am trying to fix my own hair. Go ask Toby."

"No, she is grumpy this morning."

"Then go eat your breakfast, and I can fix it when I am done."

"I already ate," I told her.

Now a little exacerbated, she looks at me and says, "I don't know what to tell you; you will have to wait."

Just then, Arthur enters the room whistling with my mother's clothes ironed and ready for church. He is happy as always. He looks at me and says, "What's wrong with you, Peanut Butt," a nickname he has recently given me.

I said, "I need help with my hair."

He said, "Can I try?"

I handed him the brush reluctantly, unsure of his ability to complete the task at hand.

He smiles intuitively, knowing I am doubting his abilities.

He very gently combs my hair, starting from the bottom and slowly working his way up to the top so it doesn't hurt too bad. My mother instructs him to wet the brush so he can tame the cowlick on the back right side of my head. After several tries, he finally finagles my hair into a ponytail with only a couple of small lumps; attempting to smooth them down, he turns me toward the mirror and, with a triumphant smile, says, "There, done."

I examined my hair and did not have the heart to tell him, "Mommy does it better." I simply, and as politely as I can, mumble out a thank you.

He calls out to my mother, "Hey, Deb, how does this look?" He must have done an okay job, or my mother was running really behind and didn't have the time to fix it because she gave it her seal of approval.

I walk over to the couch and find Brandi watching cartoons. I plop myself beside her a little too close, but she doesn't seem to notice or mind. I put my thumb in my mouth and twirl my ponytail as I watch the cartoons, waiting to head to church. I drift in thought as I think about my life and how much it has changed. Things are very different these days since Mommy married Arthur. We moved to a different city. I can no longer just walk with my sisters to my Gammy's house. Our new house is gray and in a neighborhood with lots of other houses. I haven't had a chance to meet anyone yet. But I like the idea of something new. It is fun and adventurous. I still share a room with my sister Brandi, and Toby has made the garage into her room. I am happy, and so is my mommy.

My mom and Arthur walk into the living room with a

load of stuff in hand. "Time to go," they announce. I get up off the couch and head for the car parked outside. The car was a small tan hatchback that played a special kind of tape I had never seen before. We all piled in and found our spot. I got in the middle without protest because I knew that was where I would end up. Arthur put the car in reverse and back out of the driveway. He turned and squeezed my knee before putting it into drive. I squirmed and giggled; he always seemed to know how to lighten my mood. He laughed and started driving to church.

Children's church was fun, as always. I have a lot of new friends now. I know all the songs, and I am starting to really understand the stories they tell. Snack time is my favorite time, but so are the puppet shows and arts and crafts. When Arthur talks about Jesus, I have this desire to know Him as he does, but I never say a word. I just listen and take it all in. Today, as the service is getting close to the end, Arthur asks if anyone wants to ask Jesus into their heart, to raise their hand with everyone's eyes closed and every head bowed. I want to, but I am scared, so my hand stays at my side. Arthur prays for a few of the children who want to ask Jesus into their hearts. Nothing extravagant happens; they just smile and go back to their seats. I can't help but wonder what it's all about. He dismisses the service. We start to clean up and put things back the way they were like we do every Sunday. Just as we are finishing, Arthur runs up behind me and grabs me and tosses me into the air, then lugs me over his shoulder like a bag of potatoes. I laugh uncontrollably as he says, "Let's go home and eat; I am starving."

On the car ride home, everyone is quiet in thought. I look over at Brandi, and she has fallen asleep with her head against the glass. I look over, and Toby is staring off with her face all scrunched. I put my thumb in my mouth, rest my head on Brandi's shoulder, and twirl my hair with my fingers. I must have fallen asleep because the next thing I remember is the car parked in our driveway and everyone getting out of the car. I get up, and my mother asks me to help get some stuff out of the car. I walk around to the back of the car and take what I am able and head to the house. I put the stuff down and lie on the couch and turn the TV on to cartoons; my eyes are very heavy, and before I know it, I am drifting back off to sleep.

I am awakened by the smell of food. It smells so heavenly. I sit up on the couch and rub my eyes. My ponytail is loose and lopsided. I grab my ponytail and split it in two and pull it tight in the hope of tightening and straightening it. I can hear my mother and Arthur in the kitchen. My mother is cooking, and Arthur is setting the table. As I walk around the corner, Arthur's eyes light up, and he says, "Well, hey, sleepy head." I smiled and said hi. He said, "Are you hungry?"

I shook my head yes, walking over to my mother to see what she made.

"Yum, chicken and noodles with corn, my favorite," I said.

My mother laughed and said, "Everything is your favorite, silly girl."

"How much longer?" I whined.

"About ten minutes," she replied.

I walked over to my spot at the table and waited. Slowly but surely, everyone made their way to the table for supper. Mom made my plate and set it in front of me. I waited as everyone got their food and sat down at the table. Arthur said, "Okay, let's pray." He thanked the Lord for all of us coming into his life and prayed that the Lord would bless and sanctify the food and then closed with amen. We all started to eat. I put a spoonful in my mouth, then spit it out immediately. "Ouch, that was hot," I protested. As I blow on my food, I look over at Arthur, who is almost done, and I haven't even started. He eats very fast; he says it is because he was in the Navy, and they only had a short amount of time to eat their food. But, even when he finishes first, he always stays at the table and talks with us until we are all finished.

Once supper was over, Toby, Brandi, and I had to clear the table, wash the dishes, and wipe down the counters. We all would clear the table together, and then Toby would wash the dishes, and then Brandi would dry them and put them away. I would wipe down the counters. Tonight, as I was wiping the counters, Toby came over and said, "You are not doing it right. Here, let me show you. You have to catch the food with your hand and take it to the trash and then spray and wipe the counters off so there is nothing left behind." So I grabbed the rag and started wiping the food into my hand and then taking it to the trash. Grabbing the spray, I spray the table and wipe carefully to get every spot. I hand the rag to Toby, and as I leave the kitchen, I notice she is at the table, wiping it again. *I must have missed a spot*, I think to myself.

My mother yells for me to get ready for my bath from her room. I love bath time. I get my Barbie doll and my clothes to sleep in and then head to the bathroom, where my mother already has the water running for me. *Yay, bubbles! I love bubbles*, I think as I get into the tub.

I am playing when Arthur comes in and says, "You

almost done? Have you washed your hair?"

I shake my head no. I said, "Can you wash my hair?"

He says, "Sure." He grabs a cup from the rim of the tube and instructs me to lean my head back. I do as I am told. After my hair is wet, he applies the shampoo and then rinses that out too. As he put the conditioner in my hair, I started asking for Mr. Washcloth. Mr. Washcloth has a special voice and washes me in a silly manner. Mr. Washcloth always makes me giggle. "Okay, all clean," Arthur says. "Let's rinse that conditioner out of your hair, and you are all done." He grabs the towel. "And now you can go get your pajamas on for bed."

I head to my room to get dressed. I start with my underwear. They are hard to get on because my body is still a little wet. My mommy walks into the room and says, "Here, let me help you." She grabs the towel and starts drying my hair the rest of the way. She grabs my top and helps me slip it on over my head. Then she grabs my pants and helps me put one leg in at a time. "Do you want me to comb your hair?" she asks. I shook my head yes in reply. She walks out of the bedroom and returns with a brush. She pats a spot on the bed for me to sit. She carefully brushes my hair from top to bottom to get all the tangles out. She gently kisses me on my head. "I love you," she says.

I hug her as hard as I can, "I love you too, Mommy." I crawl into bed and lay my head on my pillow. She pulls the covers over me and turns off my light. As she is leaving the room, I ask her to have Arthur come to my room.

As I wait for Arthur's arrival, I drift into deep thought. I am thinking about all the things he has been teaching in church and how he said that Jesus died for me so that I may live. I know that Jesus must be real because He made my mom happy again. Plus, I remember when I met Arthur, there was something so different about him, and even now, there is a light in him. He is so gentle and kind. I know it must be because of Jesus. At that moment, I decide I must have this Jesus too. I want to know Him as Arthur knows Him. As Arthur walks through my door, a smile lights up my face. I jump up out of bed and put my arms around his neck. He hugs me back.

"What is it?" he asks me as he places me back into bed.

I said, "I just love you."

He said, "Well, I love you too. Your mother said you asked me to come in here; she said you wanted me."

"Yes," I replied. "Will you pray for me like you did last night?"

He said, "Well, of course," with a huge smile on his

face.

"But before you start, I have one request."

"Okay, what is it?" he asked.

"I want to ask Jesus into my heart."

Arthur froze in his spot, and I could see tears in his eyes. "Lindsy, of course, I will pray with you." He kneeled down beside my bed and grabbed my hands. He instructed me to close my eyes and told me to repeat after him; I quickly complied.

The prayer went something like this: "Lord, I come to You today and ask that You forgive me of all my sins, change me, and make me new. Lord, I ask You to come into my heart and fill me with Your Spirit and make me brand new. In Jesus' name, I pray. Amen."

Once I was done reciting this prayer, he said, "All done."

I sat there for a minute to see if anything was different or if I could feel some guy in my heart. After a few seconds, I realize I don't really feel any different. Arthur leans over and kisses my forehead and tells me goodnight. "Good night, Arthur, and thank you."

Lying in my bed, I notice I feel very peaceful and warm. Not afraid to drift asleep like I usually am. I turn to my side and close my eyes and think about what Jesus looks like, where He is, and if He knows my name. I think about heaven and the angels. I wonder if Adam and Eve have a belly button or if I have my very own guardian angel. How did Noah get all those animals on the boat, and how did they not all eat each other? How did Moses part the Red Sea? Before I knew it, I was fast asleep with my thoughts on heavenly places.

This was my first encounter with Jesus; I was able to come to Him as a small child. I felt safe enough in the environment my parents had set for me. They paved the way for me through their godly example and unconditional love. I had a voice, and I used it. Bold and fearless, I met salvation with my daddy guiding the way. It still brings tears to my face even now.

The years up to this point were what I like to think of as my lighter days when things were innocent, and I learned about love and family despite my beginnings. Our family was finally complete, and the world seemed safe and peaceful. I was full of life and never knew a stranger. I was safe in the safe place that my family had created for me. What I didn't know was the years to come would be the beginning of the darker years and would change my life and perspective forever.

"Behold, I stand at the door and knock. If anyone hears My voice and opens the door, I will come in to him and dine with him, and he with Me" (Revelation 3:20, NKJV).

Chapter 8

1987: THE SECOND ATTEMPT

"But whoever causes one of these little ones who believe in Me to sin, it would be better for him if a millstone were hung around his neck, and he were drowned in the depth of the sea."

—Matthew 18:6 (NKJV)

"Mommy, can we go to Walmart yet? I need to get Bernice a present for the party," I whined impatiently.

"Do you know what you want to get her?"

"Yes, I thought about it all week, so can we go now?"

My mother patiently looked at me and said, "The party doesn't start until 2 p.m., and it's only 9 a.m."

I let out an exaggerated sigh and said, "But I want to get her present now. I am so excited."

My mother patted my head and grabbed her purse and said, "Okay, if it means that much to you, we can go get it now."

I jumped up and down, screaming with excitement. We head to the car.

My mother says, "Remember we can only spend fifteen dollars for the present; money is tight this month."

I hear her but am too preoccupied to acknowledge her; knowing, my mom just smiles and gets into the car. I jumped into the back seat, buckled up, and looked out the window as my momma started the car and headed to Walmart.

When we arrive, I jump out of the car and start running to the entrance when my mother yells for me to wait on her. I stop and impatiently wait for her to catch up. She grabs my hand, and I drag her to the toy section. I ran right up to the section that held just what I was looking for. I found the perfect My Little Pony, pink with purple hair. *Yes*, I thought to myself as I saw the price was only $9.99.

"That leaves enough money left over for wrapping," my mother says.

Proud of myself for finding the perfect gift at the right price, I look to my mother and say, "Let's go get the gift bag."

She gave me the present and led me to the wrapping section, where we took our time looking through the gift bags and finally decided to get a pink bag with purple tissue paper to match the gift inside.

When we got home, my mother helped me put the present in the bag and showed me how to do the tissue paper in a special way so that you cannot see the present inside; you scrunch the paper to look kinda like a fountain of paper and then place it along the top. When we were done, it looked amazing, and I was so super proud of what I would be bringing to the party. I looked at my mother and squeezed her neck.

"I love you, Mommy," I said.

She gently lifted me off the ground and stood me up and said, "I love you too, baby." My mother instructed me to just relax and watch some TV because I still had several hours until the birthday party started; I reluctantly complied.

I turned on the TV to my favorite cartoon and lay down sideways on the couch, put my thumb in my mouth, and began to twirl my hair; as I lay there watching cartoons and sucking my thumb, I drifted off in thoughts of the party. It was my very first pool party at a friend's house, and I absolutely loved to swim. The time seemed to go by so slowly. Every time I looked at the clock, expecting it to be almost time, it would only be five minutes later than the time I looked before. I am not sure when, but at some point, I drifted off to sleep because the next thing I knew, my mother was sitting beside me on the couch, softly whispering my name. I jolt up with excitement, realizing it must be time. My mother said, "Go get your bathing suit on and your bag of clothes along with your gift; Bernice is waiting." I jump up and run to my room. I find my favorite bathing suit laid out on the bed for me. I quickly take my clothes off and put my bathing suit on, followed by a tank top and shorts my mother put out for me too. I grabbed my bag and the present and ran to the living room, where my mom was waiting for me with a sweet smile on her face. She stands up and says, "Let's go," knowing I was beyond ready.

Bernice's house is only a few minutes away, within driving distance, but it seems to take an eternity. As we arrive, I can see other kids running up to the front door. I am so beyond myself at this point; my very first birthday party, and it's a pool party to boot! I turn toward my mother and give her a kiss. I then open my car door, bolting for the house, when all of a sudden, I hear my mother yell my name. I freeze and turn to see her holding the present up in the window for me to see that I had forgotten it. I turn around, slightly embarrassed I forgot it. I run back and grab it from her, then quickly head toward the house, giving a swift backward wave as I go through the front door.

As I enter the door, I see Bernice immediately; I walk over to her with a huge grin on my face and hand her her present. She takes it and hands it to her mother as she says thank you. She grabs my hand and leads me to her room so she can get ready for her party. I feel honored; as the rest of her guests have to wait for her at the pool, I get to hang with her in her room while she finishes getting ready. She is so excited and talking super fast that I can barely keep up with what she is saying. She finally emerges from her closet, where she was putting her swimsuit on, and she looks at me and frowns.

"What?" I ask. "Why are you looking at me like that?"

She said, "You're not ready. You still have your clothes on over your bathing suit. Don't you want to go swimming?" she asked.

That was the moment I realized I was nervous and shy. I smiled and took off my clothes, leaving me in my bathing suit so as not to disappoint my friend. She leads me out of her room toward the pool in the backyard. The house smells like yummy food; I look toward the kitchen as we pass, and I see her mother and father cooking our supper.

I smile a shy smile and continue to the pool. By the time we make it to the pool, I am a little more comfortable in my lack of clothing, and I am ready to join all the other kids in the water. There were so many, like fifteen kids; *I never had a birthday party with this many kids*, I thought to myself. Just then, Bernice jumps in the water, yelling, "Come on," over her shoulder at me. On cue, I let out a squeal and leaped in.

We played so many water games like Marco Polo, Find the Treasures, pool volleyball, above-the-water and below-the-water races, and who could hold their breath the longest. It was so much fun. We were carefree, and time just seemed to fly by. I was just about to take my turn in how far I could swim without coming up for air when Bernice's dad called my name. I looked up, and he was making a phone shape with his hand. He spoke very little English, so I understood the gesture that I had a phone call. I got out of the pool and told them I would be right back. I grabbed a towel and dried off as quickly as I could and headed into the house. I saw her dad sitting in the hallway with the phone. I walked up to him, and he motioned for me to sit on his lap, so I did; at this point, I was very uneasy, but I just couldn't figure out why my heart was racing so fast. I grabbed the phone from his hand and said hello. That's when I heard a fast, busy sound, *beep-beep-beep.* I handed him the phone and said, "No one is there."

He smiled and looked at me and said, "Kiss."

I was confused but did not want to be rude, so I leaned in to kiss his cheeks, ignoring the alarms going off in my body.

He leaned back and said, "No, like this," and he stuck his tongue out and waved it back and forth. My insides were screaming; I didn't know what to do next. I was frozen and numb; my body tingled in horror. He leaned in and tried to force a kiss, and that's when I squirmed free. I was out of his grasp, and he was heading in my direction. I had to move and move fast. I ran to the pool where all the kids were, but I couldn't stop; I was too scared. I kept running; I ran past the other kids, out the screened porch, and out the backyard. I could hear Bernice yelling my name for me to come back, but I could not stop. She seemed angry, but I didn't stop running till I could see my house in the distance.

When I arrived home, no one was there. I was so grateful because I needed time to think about what happened. I was cold down to my core, I was shaking, so I went into the bathroom and turned the faucet on mostly hot, and plugged the hole so the bath could fill up. I could see the steam start to rise up; I knew the temperature would be perfect for the bone-crushing cold I felt. I slowly began to remove my bathing suit and let it fall to the floor; I just stood there for a second. I was too numb to do anything fast. I slowly lowered myself into the water, immersing my whole body except my nose and mouth. I just lay there for what seemed like an eternity until the warmth returned to my bones. I tried to cry, but tears never came.

I just sat there forever, playing the events of the day in my head, the moments leading up to what happened. I thought, *Did I smile too big? Did I say something I shouldn't have? Did I imply that I wanted this in some way? Should I have left my tank top on?* I found no answers to my questions, only more questions. After a while, I came to the conclusion the only thing to do was to say nothing and to never go back to my friend's house again. I got out of the bath, dried off with a towel as best I could, got my clothes on, and went to the living room. I grabbed the remote control and flipped through the channels until I found some cartoons. I made a conscious decision to put the day as deep as it could go so it would not ever come up again; strangely, it wasn't that hard.

My mother woke me up from my slumber when she returned home. She said, "What are you doing? I went to pick you up, and they said you went home and left your stuff behind." I hated the way she was looking at me with concern. "Why would you leave your stuff behind like that, Lindsy? You know clothes are not cheap." I looked up into my mother's yellow eyes, and for a second, I almost told her everything that occurred that day in the hallway with a man I didn't even know who was three times my age, but the filthy shame overcame me, and I swallowed the day back down forcing it back into its new home. And when I found the courage to speak again, I looked her in the eyes, and I said my stomach hurt really bad, so I came home.

Concerned, my mother checked my temperature, which was normal, and I let out a big shiver. She asked me if I was cold, and I truthfully said yes and told her I couldn't seem to stay warm. My mother looked me over again and placed her hand on my forehead, and was now concerned I was getting sick. She grabbed me a blanket and said, "I will make you some bean and bacon soup that always helps you feel better." I let out a sigh of relief that she let the explanation stand as is and was no longer pushing for information on the events of the day. I nestled myself in the blanket and began to block out today's events from my mind. She stood and turned toward the kitchen to prepare my food, looking over her shoulder one last time with concern, and I turned my head toward the TV and let the numbness set back in.

Chapter 9

MY NEW PERSPECTIVE

"Come to Me, all you who labor and are heavy laden,
and I will give you rest."

—Matthew 11:28 (NKJV)

In an instant, my world was changed, and my innocence, lost forever. I felt what shame really felt like for the first time in my life. I was only seven years old. I had no idea how to process what happened. Even today, I cannot wrap my head around the event. I never shed a single tear that day or days to follow.

All I know is that day changed me forever. A part of my soul shattered, and the piece that shattered held that day in safety, detached from the rest of my soul so that I didn't feel the pain of it, and it helped me to remain numb. I went from being this innocent, carefree child, never meeting a stranger, trusting everyone, being the life of the party, to this person who saw bad in everyone, who was non-trusting and always waiting for the bottom to be pulled out from her at any given time. Touch had a new feeling and meaning; kindness seemed fake; people felt dangerous. I even doubted the people I was closest to, my family, and their intentions. I had no idea what to do with my thoughts and feelings, so I just continued to push them further down.

It's funny how one event, no matter how small, can change the very essence of who you are. I was suddenly a new me, and I suddenly doubted everything I was ever told or everything I ever knew to be true. This was the second attempt the devil made toward my life. The first attempt was to take me out, and when that failed, he decided to shut me up. And shut me up he did. After this, I didn't know if I was coming or going most of the time. My voice had been muted in a moment, and at the time, I wasn't sure I would ever find it again. I suddenly questioned everything, including God.

Over the next few years, this moment became more of an afterthought. I was still a changed person; my soul had aged little, and I endured many obstacles. My grandparents moved away to North Carolina, and all the things I grew up knowing were evolving as life often does. This was a very difficult time for me. I still had my mom and Arthur, but things were so different. My family had started their very own church in their home, and I was suddenly surrounded by people constantly. The thing was, this would have been great because people used to bring me energy and bring out the best in me. But not during this time. I found I always had a chip on my shoulder and was leery of everyone.

In this season of my life, I latched on to Arthur wholeheartedly because I knew he was real. I started to find my faith in God again. I would stand beside my mom and dad praying in tongues, casting out the devil, and weeping in intercession. It was the only truth I knew and trusted. My parents were all I had at this point. My sisters did their own thing, and I didn't have but a handful of friends. I even kept my friends at a distance; I could not afford to repeat the past, and I often doubted people's genuineness. But somehow, I found a new way of life, and it seemed to work for me for a little while anyway.

I was learning these nuggets from my parents on overcoming, but I did not know just how much I would need them later. As I grew closer to my parents, I became lulled to sleep by the inactivity of the devil attacking me; I found a resemblance to the peace I once had. I began to breathe again. Life was good.

Chapter 10

1991: THE THIRD ATTEMPT

"Beware of dogs, beware of evil workers, beware of the mutilation!"

—Philippians 3:2 (NKJV)

My mother entered my room as I was putting my last folded shirt on top of the stack of clothes for my trip to North Carolina. I was beyond excited. It feels like forever since I have seen Gammy and Gampy. I was a little nervous because I had never flown before, and I was doing it alone. My mother assures me the flight attendant will be with me the whole time and that it is a straight flight. So, that means when I land, my Gammy will be waiting for me. I took a deep breath to calm my nerves. I would miss my mom and dad so much, but I really needed a break and couldn't wait to see the people who helped raise me.

My mom handed me a suitcase and began to help me pack it so that everything fit just right. Then she began to go through the list of things I would need, like toothbrush and toothpaste, to make sure I forgot nothing. In the end, I did forget to pack my brush and hair ties, but that's why we went through the list. She closed the suitcase and put it by the door. She gently gave me a hug and told me to go to bed because the flight left early in the morning. I did as I was told. I brushed my teeth, kissed my mom and dad goodnight, and went to bed. Surprisingly, I found sleep quickly, and dreams of this summer flashed across my mind like the big screen in the movies.

I was awakened by my father's gentle whisper of my name, and I sat up in bed. He put his finger over his mouth to remind me to be quiet and not wake my sister. I put on the clothes I laid out the night before, brushed my teeth, and fixed my hair. I walked out into the kitchen, where my dad was getting the fixings of my cereal ready for me. I asked where Mom was, and he said, "I thought I would let her sleep in a little later before we left." But he assured me she would be joining us today to the airport. I was instantly relieved as I wanted both my parents to see me off. I knew I was going to miss them so much, but I was so grateful they were letting me go.

I was washing my cereal bowl from breakfast when my mother came around the corner, beautiful as ever, dressed and ready to go. She came over to me, gave me a slight squeeze, and said, "I am going to miss you so much." I knew exactly how she felt: happy I got to go but sad because she was going to miss me. I assured her I would be okay and that I would come back with lots of stories to tell. I knew my Gammy and Gampy were taking me all over camping and tubing and visiting relatives I didn't know. A lot of adventures were in store.

My parents and I headed for the car with bags at hand. We loaded up and headed toward the airport. The ride to the airport was pretty quiet, as we were all lost in our own thoughts. It was getting light outside the closer to the airport we got, and by the time we arrived, the sun was shining bright to light the way. My parents got me checked in and handed me over to the attendant when they reached as far as they could go; as I walked away, I turned my head over my shoulder one last time before they were out of sight to remember the moments and take it all in. Little did I know that was the last time I would see them through rose-stained glasses because my innocence would be lost even further on this trip. My innocence would be lost worse than before on this trip, and yet it wasn't as bad as what was to come. We smiled and waved goodbye to one another, and then they were gone.

The attendant helps me find my seat before anyone else

is able to board. She lifts my carry-on and places it in the overhead compartment for me. She instructs me to put my seatbelt on and then leaves to begin the process of boarding the other passengers. I am staring out my window when I realize just how jittery I feel. I have never flown before. What if it crashes? What if Gammy and Gampy forget to pick me up? Trying to settle my nerves, I close my eyes and think about all the adventures that are in store when I arrive, and that seems to do the trick, at least for now.

I am jolted to reality when I hear a voice coming on over the intercom with special instructions about masks and exits in case we crash; my heart is racing because I am afraid I will forget what she said. I am breathing a little heavier now and can't hear well. That's when I realize we are moving. I tighten my seatbelt to make sure it is latched tight. The flight attendant stops by me one last time and gently places her hand on my arm and assures me everything is going to be okay. I see her walk to her seat and buckle up. The next thing I know, we are moving faster. Now we are tilting up, my belly flips when we take off, and I hear the wheels shut up into the plane. I feel strange but a little calmer now.

They are starting to pass out drinks and snacks; relief floods my soul as food always calms me and makes me feel better. By the time snacks are over and I am done in the bathroom, a person comes on over the intercom again and instructs everyone to return to their seats and buckle up; we are preparing for landing. I do as I am told and look out the window as we get closer to landing. I can see mountains and trees that look like broccoli and clouds that look like mashed potatoes. That's when I realize just how hungry I really am. We landed without incident, and everyone began to get off the plane, starting from front to back. The attendant helped me get my bag, and I headed toward the door, doing as instructed. When I got to a certain point, that's when I saw them, my Gammy and Gampy! I didn't know how much I missed them until that moment. I ran over and gave them a hug.

Gampy patted me on the back and said, "Well, Lousy," a nickname from him, "you hungry?"

I looked up at him with a twinkle in my eye and said, "You bet." In this very moment, I was so happy and complete.

After eating at J&S Cafeteria, we headed toward their home. Waynesville is so beautiful, a small, quiet little town. We drove the backroads and just talked all the way there, listening to old-time country. In their rock driveway, there was a sign that read Almost Heaven. The house was a one-story with a basement and a wrap-around porch with a huge deck and a woodshop because my grandpa loved to build and make things with his hands. There were flowers all at the base of the porch and flowers hanging in pots from the roof of the porch. My grandma had a way with plants. Her yard always looked amazing. From the porch, you could take steps down to the basement porch, where a hot tub was, and then there was another set of stairs that led down the mountainside to a little log cabin my grandfather made with trees from the land. It was truly a piece of paradise.

I utilized this summer with my grandparents well. We went camping and tubing all over North Carolina. We visited family I did not know in West Virginia and Ohio. And when we were not actively fishing at trout farms, we were driving back roads, stopping at little mom-and-pop stores, and filling up on root beer, boiled peanuts, and cotton candy. The times we stayed home, I would either be in the hot tub or lying out on the deck. My grandfather said I reminded him of my mother at her age.

Emma was the little girl who lived close to my grandpa, and I would wait for her to come play whenever she could. She was beautiful and super sweet. We would make up little dance routines, sing, and go on adventures. Sometimes, at the end of the day, we would go have supper with her parents. Gammy and Gampy were very good friends with her parents. They would sometimes throw a party, and everyone on the mountain would come to our house and party, play pool, and hang in the hot tub. Over all, I would say that summer was amazing up to this point.

One day that summer, my Gammy summoned me to the kitchen around lunchtime and asked me if I wanted to go to Emma's birthday party that would be taking place later on that night. We would be going out to eat, then to a drive-in movie. She explained that a few other girls would also be going. I agreed excitedly; I had never been to a drive-in, and I never turn down good food. So, for the remainder of that day, until it was time to get ready, I sunbathed on the deck.

Emma called for me to walk up the hill to her house around 4:30 p.m. I was decked out in my favorite outfit. It was a black tank top, white shorts, and my black Birkenstock knockoffs. I had spent a little extra time fixing my hair and putting on a little lip gloss and mascara. I was nervous because I didn't know the other girls and wasn't sure how Emma would treat me amongst her regular friends. My nerves settled when her father eased my fears by introducing me to everyone and giving me something to drink. He also put me in the spotlight with his daughter when doing things that night so that I would not be left out.

We arrived at Shoney's to eat, and her father sat me in between him and the birthday girl that night. I thought to myself, *My grandma must have shared my fear of being left out with her parents, and they are going out of their way to make sure that didn't happen.* It wasn't till her dad and I were alone at the table that night while everyone was up getting seconds, I started feeling a strange old feeling I could not quite put my finger on. He made a comment to me about running away together and that he would take good care of me; of course, he said it jokingly, but something was a little off in the way he said it and the way he was looking at me. Instead of panicking, I brushed off my feeling as being ridiculous and reminded myself this was not the birthday party like when I was seven and that I was overreacting. I just simply giggled and smiled and went to get seconds.

We all loaded up in the cool convertible he rented for the night, and I got the privilege to sit up front with Emma. When we arrived to the drive-in, there was this huge screen and all these parking spots with a stick and a radio-type box so you could hear the movie.

Emma's parents brought blankets and two fold-out

chairs. They placed the blanket on the ground next to the car and the fold-out chairs. Some of the girls stayed in the car. Emma and I and a few other girls played on the blanket next to her parents' chairs. I honestly cannot tell you what movie we watched. We were too caught up in the adventure of it all. Laughing and talking as young girls do. Her father brought us a bunch of snacks and drinks. We were carefree and had the time of our lives.

By the time we arrived back to Emma's house, the adult party was already in full swing. Emma and the rest of us went upstairs to hang out while the adults listened to their music and did their thing. As the night grew late, a bunch of us girls crawled into bed. I somehow got stuck on the outside closest to the door. The lights were off, and we were giggling as girls often do, talking and having a good time. Just about that time, her father came in the room smelling of booze and smoking a cigarette. He came to my side of the bed with the lights still off. He started playing like he was going to get us with the cigarette. Each time, he would come close to someone different, and we would scream and squeal, and then he would repeat. The next thing I know, as he is randomly attacking the next person with the cigarette with one hand, he begins to touch me with the other hand. No one can see, and no one knows. This goes on for a while. I, at age eleven, am being touched in a way I do not understand. I am being groped and rubbed, and I grow cold. I cannot respond. My mouth is sealed shut. I am shaking and do the only thing I know to do. I shatter again and go to a secret place. And, just like that, he leaves. Finding sleep that night was almost impossible. But eventually, sleep does come.

Frightened by the sudden jolt, I awaken to someone pushing my shoulder. I do not open my eyes; I lay there playing dead, scared to death. I realize quickly he is back, and he is trying to wake me. I hear him say, "Come on, let's go somewhere." Yet, I lay there as if I was dead asleep. Eventually, he gives up and leaves. I wait to get up until all the girls awake. We walk downstairs together. I take in my surroundings and hear Emma's mother say her father left for work early this morning. Relieved, my shoulders fall with an exhale, and I do what I have done once before, and I take off for my Gammy's.

Shaken and confused, I say nothing. I take a shower and try to find warmth. Then I head to my room and dress in my pj's and dry my hair. I go over the events of the night from start to finish. Questions flooding my mind. *Did I smile too much? Did I flirt? Was it my sunbathing on my Gampy's deck? Did I give the wrong impression? Did I ask for this?* The answers never came, and just like before,

I found the strength to bury the events as far down as I could and never to think of them again. This time, it wasn't as easy; there was an apprehension and fear greater than before. I pulled myself together and headed to the kitchen where my grandparents were and put the best smile I could muster across my face. I ate lunch in silence and then made my way to the couch. As the day led to night and my grandparents went to sleep, I found myself watching a movie in utter fear. I locked all the doors and positioned myself in a way I could see all the entrances to the house. I knew my friend's father had a key to my grandparents' house, and I was beyond afraid he would come to finish the job. I did not fall asleep until my grandparents woke up and started their day. Even then, I am not sure I slept much.

That man never showed up, never spoke to me again, never apologized. He just went on with his life as if nothing ever happened. I learned something very valuable that night. Silence. Silence saved me, not from everything, but it saved me the next morning. I can't even imagine what would have happened to me had I opened my eyes and responded to his shoves. This was just another ploy from the enemy to keep me quiet, and it was working. At this point in my life, I felt like I could not bear any more, and yet the worst was yet to come. I had grabbed ahold of the lie of the devil, and I was sinking fast. At this point, I could not even find the words to pray. I was lost, scared, and confused.

Chapter 11

LIFE AFTER THE FACT

"But those who wait on the Lord Shall renew their strength; They shall mount up with wings like eagles, They shall run and not be weary, They shall walk and not faint."

—Isaiah 40:31 (NKJV)

We all have a story and something that we have gone through. Everyone's stories are different. Some are bad, and some are good. I was given the tools at a young age to deal with life. I was instructed to love and have faith and to cast all my cares upon Jesus. Even with two very loving parents and a strong foundation in Christ, I was not prepared on how to deal with a shattered soul.

I was once so loving and caring, never met a stranger, and truly thrived off being in the presence of others. To now, at this point, leery of everyone. I second-guessed all of my actions; I second-guessed everyone's intentions when they spoke to me. I was a broken and empty shell. I had shattered and placed the good pieces of me into safe places so no one could hurt them ever again. I was now a brass and abrasive little girl with a giant chip on her shoulder and ready to throw down. It was my protective mechanism. I hated who I was and who I had become.

I loved my family, but they were the only ones I loved and trusted. After all, they had never done anything to hurt me the way that others had. I loved God but questioned if He really cared for me. The next few years following the third attempt to silence me were very dark and lonely times. I withdrew from everyone I loved. I kept everyone on a superficial level. Only allowing people to see glimpses of the real me. I just glued myself to video games and the few friends I had.

However, God was not done with me yet. He had a plan and a purpose for me, and He was not going to give up on me yet. In 1993, only two years later, He sent another jewel into my life that would forever change my course, even if I didn't realize it until now. My life would have great trials, but I would have a rock to support me through it all. I am eternally grateful for this precious gift.

Chapter 12

1993: THE DAY I MET HIM

"I waited patiently for the Lord; And He inclined to me, And heard my cry."

—Psalm 40:1 (NKJV)

As I place the last slice of cheese into the sauce to melt for my tuna casserole, my mother calls out my name. I stir the sauce, careful not to let it stick to the bottom of the pan. I add my noodles that had been draining and stir it all together for a final masterpiece. I place it all in a bowl, grab a spoon, and head to my mother's bathroom, where I heard her call me from. I come around the corner and see her gently spraying her hair with hairspray as she has it suspended in the air and then curling it down in an attempt for the perfect bang wave.

Our eyes meet, and she says, "Lindsy, you are not ready."

"Ready for what?" I replied.

We are going to the church to meet the family who is coming to play music for us this week. I placed a large spoonful of the tuna casserole in my mouth and said, "What does that have to do with me?" She proceeded to tell me they have children my age, and she really wants me to be there. I sigh in irritation at the fact this is really messing with my dinner and reluctantly walk toward my bedroom to get dressed.

After scarfing my dinner down, I jumped in the shower and started getting ready for the meeting. I put on nothing fancy as I preferred comfort over beauty. I brushed my teeth and dragged my feet like any thirteen-year-old would do. I just wanted to play *Zelda* in my own peaceful company. I walk into the living room to my mother gathering her keys and motioning for me to come on.

I asked, "Where is Arthur?"

"He will meet us there," she said.

I slowly make my way to the car with my mother's frustration mounting. I closed the car door and smiled at my mom.

"What's the hurry?" I asked.

She said, "I don't like being late."

A Cheshire-like grin crept on my face as if I didn't already know the answer to the questions. We drove in silence the rest of the way to church.

My parents' church was in a little strip mall; it wasn't much, but it was their heartbeat, blood, sweat, and tears. I really admired them for all the work they did and for how much they really stood by what they believed in. They were amazing role models. We pulled up into the parking space closest to the entrance. I get out of the car, shut the door behind me, and head for the front door. The closer I got to the entrance, I could hear music, but what mainly stood out to me was the sound of the drums. Up until this point, my parents just used tapes for music, so I wasn't used to live pumping music even though I had heard it before. I grab the handle, and I am strangely excited; I feel butterflies, but I have no idea why. I walk in, and the sound of the music is so loud it slaps me across the face; it takes me a minute to gain my composure and to realize where I am. I look toward the direction of the noise, and that is when I see it. A beautiful big set of royal blue drums, they were the most beautiful set of drums I have ever seen. What happens next will change my life forever. As I was admiring the drums, I noticed a hand, and the hand led to an arm, and as I traced the arm, I found the face. The boy's name was Robert Alex Cummings, but everyone called him Robby, and he was the most beautiful specimen of a man I had ever seen. Our eyes met, and he gave me a cute half smile, and I knew, right then and there, I was gonna marry that boy someday. And so I did only two years later.

It was young love, passionate, exciting, and bold. We were attracted to each other like magnets. His parents stayed in town for a while, and by the end of their stay, Robby refused to return home. He was in love and found shelter with a friend and his wife, and our relationship grew stronger from there. We were inseparable. I had found my compass, my true north. My past seemed to vanish from the forefront of my mind, and peace had returned. I wouldn't trade a single second of our first year together. The memories are some of the best memories of my life.

Robby had dark brown hair cut in a mullet style. Big brown eyes and almost feminine-like features, which were in complete contrast to my masculine-like features, light brown hair, and blue eyes. We were complete opposites in every way imaginable. I was loud, spastic, spontaneous, brass, abrasive, impulsive, quick to anger, flighty, adventurous, and always wanting to try something new. He was quiet, calm, gentle, kind, slow to move, slow to anger, steadfast, grounded. He was everything I was not, and I was everything he was not. He was everything I didn't know I needed and more.

Robby had a gentle kindness to his eyes. I am not sure how, but I just knew he would love me no matter what. I became friends with his sister and got really close to his family. The closer I got to Robby, the more I began to hope that maybe, just maybe, I could have a normal life like everyone else. I slowly allowed myself to hope for a better future. He was loving and protective and always wanted me by his side. He was ready to marry me at thirteen, but of course, I was not ready. He was an old soul, quiet and gentle. I craved the essence of who he was. I wanted to feel again, to love again, to trust again. Somehow, he was able to cross over my outer walls and melt away the ice deep within my bones.

He was so talented, and as time passed by, I struggled with insecurities and jealousy. He was so beautiful and was in the limelight. Every girl around wanted to be with him. And even though he assured me I was all he could see, there was a deep root seed of distrust to all men. And I just knew he was going to let me down. I struggled with myself and my relationship with Robby for many years to come. He was too perfect; at some point, the bottom was going to come out; I could just feel it. Little did I know the bottom was not going to be him hurting me but a much deeper pain, and God was going to use Robby to show me love and forgiveness.

He always put me first. He would work every day hard like a dog, and even before he went home to shower, he would pick me up from school, take me to get something to eat, and then take me to the house and just hang out with me. He had a way of always making me laugh, even if I was in a bad mood or depressed. He had a way of cheering me up and making me smile and helping me to connect with life again. That is one of the reasons I was so drawn to him. I needed that.

His parents were very cautious of me, and rightfully so. I was broken, lost, and hurting. And as the story goes, hurt people hurt people even if it is not their intent. My relationship with his sister became more and more strained the closer I got to Robby. I broke it off with Robby several times through the course of our relationship, but he was like a bulldog, never letting go. Always fighting for me. Sometimes, I wonder if he would have fought so hard if he had been able to see the future.

In retrospect, I feel like I should have turned around, walked out of that church, and gone back to playing my games. Maybe I could have prevented him from all the pain and heartache I was unknowingly going to put him through. I did not know at the time that my journey was only going to grow darker and that this newfound hope was going to be short-lived. He deserved so much more than I could give.

He deserved so much more than the hell I was going to put him through, but then God. God knew the beginning, the middle, and the end. He knew what our story would be together. He knew I needed him so much more than I even knew. He knew that our story would one day lead to the healing of the brokenhearted. Even now, tears come at the thought of His knowing and the gift of Him giving me what I needed, not what I wanted. The road ahead would be very long and hard, but I can honestly say one hundred percent worth it.

Chapter 13

1994: THE FORTH ATTEMPT

"Be sober, be vigilant; because your adversary the devil walks about like a roaring lion, seeking whom he may devour."

—1 Peter 5:8 (NKJV)

"I am tired," I said in a high-pitched complaining whine. "I don't feel like going to church tonight. It's been a long week, and I have to go to school in the morning. Please don't make me go. I just want to chill out and watch mind-numbing TV and go to bed at a decent hour," I protest to my mother. My father had already left for the Sunday night service, and I was giving my mother a very hard time about going to church, which was oddly out of character for me. But since I had recently broken up with Robby, I am having a hard time seeing him, his sad puppy eyes; it breaks my heart, and I just need to breathe a little. I walk into my mother's bathroom and lock eyes with her, pleading to give me just one pass. She reluctantly concedes; triumphantly, I hug her neck and kiss her cheek. I walk to my room, and as I open the door, the smell of sun-ripened raspberries takes over my senses. I walk to my desk and blow out the candle that has made my room smell so heavenly. My room is clean, and everything is in the place it should be. I pull open my top drawer and grab my pajamas. I walk over to my bed, undress, and put my pj's on; total comfort. I smile and walk to the kitchen. I put a frozen pizza in the microwave. While I am waiting for that to be done, I walk over to grab a glass from the cabinet and then grab the sweet tea from the refrigerator. As I am pouring my glass of tea, the microwave dings. I grab my pizza and my sweet tea and head for the living room.

I position myself on the couch, place my pizza in my lap and my tea on the end table, grab the remote, and begin to channel surf as my mother walks into the living room. She looks beautiful, makeup and hair perfect, and she smells like my mom always did. She leans down and kisses me on the cheek and says, "I will be back soon. Lock the door, don't let anyone in." I agreed, got up, and locked the door behind my mother. I walked over to the couch and positioned myself as before and started surfing the channels again until I found something suitable to watch.

Side note: While I am watching mind-numbing TV at

home, my parents are at the church dealing with a very uncomfortable situation, one I do not find out about until several years later. A twenty-two-year-old man by the name of George came into the church several weeks ago from a place my dad had been affiliated with. This man had many demons. In weeks leading up to this night, he had been doing very odd and strange things. For one thing, he did a word fast. He would not speak to anyone. If you spoke to him, he would get his tablet out and write a reply. His strangeness continued to grow and came to a head that night. While I was at home vegging out watching TV, he was at the church being reprimanded. Through a course of events, he was asked to leave the church that night, and he did. Little did I know our paths were about to collide as a retaliation to my father. My father passed away never knowing the truth of the events that happened that night.

I was almost asleep when I heard the doorknob turn. I sat up, my mind still pretty foggy. I saw him at the door, and he smiled at me. I was confused. I was not sure why he was there, but maybe he was looking for my father. Maybe he missed church and wanted to talk to my dad. It wasn't until I unlocked the door to crack it that I realized I had made a grave mistake. He pushed his way into my living room. I didn't speak; I was frozen. He had a craziness to his eyes. He almost didn't look human. I walked toward the couch and sat down. I was terrified. I thought I was going to die. I wasn't ever going to see the people I love ever again. Would they be able to find me? Would they know how much I cared for them? He slowly walks around the couch and stands in front of me. He grabs my arm to make me stand. I try to pull my arm away, and he tightens his grip. I look up, and his eyes are empty. He has a crazy grin on his face. I began to shiver. The all-too-familiar coldness has returned. I cannot feel my hand, my body, just the violent shivers. He seems to notice that I am violently shivering and lets out an eerie laugh. He pulls me to my feet. I cannot feel my body; it is very hard to walk. I am being dragged to my bedroom. I think to myself, *This is it. God, please let my family and Robby know how much I love them. Help them to locate my body.* He closes the door behind me, and my torment begins. I will not give the details after this, but I will say this: I was raped, frozen in fear, and numb. I somehow was able to separate myself from the trauma. My soul shattered once again in a vain attempt to protect me. I lost my mind that night; I lost me. When he was done, he let out a wicked laugh, looked me in the eyes, and said, "Now you have all my demons." He put his clothes back on and walked out of my house like nothing ever happened.

I lay there for what seemed like an eternity. I could

not move. I could not cry. I just lay there naked and violently shivering. So many thoughts were going through my mind. *I should not have opened the door. I was too friendly, too flirty in prior dealings with him. Did I dress too inappropriately? Did I ask for this? What could I have done differently? I should have gone to church.* Once I could think no more, I got up and took myself to the shower and scrubbed my body as hard as I could. An old familiar sadness returned, and my universe turned dark and cold. By the time I got out of the shower, I felt nothing. I put on new pajamas, threw the others in the dirty clothes, crawled into bed, and went to sleep with a vacant mind. I knew as I drifted off to sleep I would never speak of this night to anyone. The shame was too large to bear.

The following morning, I got up, got dressed, and went to school. I was numb and playing the role of perfect Lindsy the best I could. I laughed at jokes on cue even though I did not feel the laughter. I smiled and spoke to people when spoken to. I was going through the motions but not feeling anything. I made it through day one. I got home and watched TV until I knew Robby would be home. I called him and asked him to come over to my house. I needed to feel something, anything, and he was the only one who could do it if it could be done. He came over and hung out with me; I just soaked up his sweetness. I told him I wanted to be with him again, and he was so happy. We made plans for that weekend; we were going to go to the movies. I thought the worst was over, and now I can just pick up the pieces like before and move on with my life. Boy, was I dead wrong.

Robby came by after school on Friday to pick me up. I was at peace knowing I was safe as long as I was with him. We went and got something to eat and then headed to my house so I could get ready for our movie. I came out of my room dressed in blue jeans and a flannel shirt. Robby was talking to my mom, and he looked so happy; I knew then I would never make him carry this burden. He was the part of me untouched by the darkness I radiated. I smiled at them both and said I was ready. I jumped up in the middle of his little black Isuzu truck as close as I could to him. He turned his truck on and pushed play to his CD player. We just listened to Counting Crows all the way there. No need for words. I was lost in thought. I can't even recall the movie we watched. But what I do recall is what happened after the movie. I went to the payphone to call my mom and let her know the movie was over and I would be home soon.

Her voice stopped me in my tracks. It was calm and controlled. She said, "Lindsy, I have something to tell you," and my body froze with chills going up my spine. She said, "Lindsy, do you remember George from the deliverance center?"

I heard my voice reply yes, but I don't remember moving my lips.

She swallowed and said, "Well, he has been arrested."

I felt the earth spinning, and I couldn't make it stop. I steady myself and muster up the courage to say, "Why?"

She said, "Well, when he left here a few Sundays ago, he drove home a few states away and stabbed his fiancée multiple times with a pair of carpet scissors."

I gasped and breathed, "Is she dead?"

My mother replied, "No, she is in the ICU in critical condition."

I hung up the phone with my mother and acted as normal as I could. I looked at Robby and said I was ready to go home. All the way home, we drove in silence, drowned out by the loud music. My thoughts, exploding with fear, sadness, and hate. Fear that he would return to finish me off one day, sadness for the women in the ICU, and hate because it was all my fault; I did nothing to stop him.

I did this. This is my fault. If I had only fought back,

I would be dead, and she would be okay. It would have stopped with me. Or if I had only spoken up and told them what happened to me, he may have been stopped before he left, and she would be okay. No matter what way I spun it, her life and what she went through was all my fault. I carried this burden for years to come. After that, I became a dark human being. I trusted no one. That week changed my life forever. I felt like I was treading in a very large body of water with my head just high enough to breathe and my strength leaving me. I didn't know how much time I had left.

Chapter 14

PICKING UP THE PIECES

"The Lord is near to those who have a broken heart,
And saves such as have a contrite spirit."

—Psalm 34:18 (NKJV)

I found myself in a place wrapped in chains of guilt and shame. My life was in shambles; I was scared and alone. I had shut off all of my emotions; I trusted no one and nothing. I was standing in a room full of people, all of whom I knew very well, and I felt utterly alone. No one had a clue what I had gone through, and I was completely okay with that. In fact, I preferred it. I could trust no one, including myself. Everything was my fault, making it my burden to bear.

During this time, I began to draw myself closer to Robby's side. I think, subconsciously, I felt he could keep me the safest if George ever returned. I also felt the calmest around Robby. He had a way of calming the raging sea within me just by being in the room. I never understood it;

I just allowed it because I needed peace any way I could get it. He didn't even have to try.

The closer I got to Robby, the more his parents seemed to hate me. I didn't care. I needed him. I was hanging on for dear life, and he was my only sanity. I hated myself and everything I stood for. I had come to the realization that I had a sign on my forehead that read, "Come and attack me, rape me, touch me. I am the perfect victim." And come hell or high water, I would never be a victim again. I was a basket case, jealous, insecure, non-trusting, and prone to fits of rage. No matter how I acted, Robby stayed. He would talk me down and bring me peace when I was at my most confused. I loved and hated him for it.

I was somehow able to pick up the pieces of my shattered soul and live the resemblance of what appeared to be a normal life. But, oh, how broken I really was. The following years, though challenging, would be what I referred to as my quiet years. I found a way to push all the feelings deep into my soul and live life as normal as I could. I did not know at the time the deeper I pushed the feelings down and the more I allowed them to fester unchecked, the larger the crater of hate, bitterness, and resentment would become, and one day in the distant future, it would all come crashing down.

Chapter 15

OCTOBER 1995

"For God has not given us a spirit of fear, but of power and of love and of a sound mind."

—2 Timothy 1:7 (NKJV)

Sitting at my desk at school, I run through my calendar one more time, sure I am wrong, sure I have missed something. I am finding it hard to breathe. My parents have been in England for a week now, and I have been staying with my Aunt Sylvia and Uncle Kee. I woke up this morning feeling very sick, and I threw up for the second time in two days. Surly, I just have the flu. There is no way it's anything else. Mrs. Elliot interrupts my thoughts with that annoying high-pitched screech of a voice she has. I turn toward her and look at her with disdain. She asks again, "Did you hand in your homework, Lindsy?" I do not answer. She speaks again, but this time much louder; I hold up my hand in a vain attempt to quiet her as I cannot bear to hear her voice anymore. I hand her my homework and turn back around in my seat. I cannot swallow back the fear I am feeling at this moment. I finally bury myself in my studies to distract myself from my thoughts. After all, there is absolutely nothing I can do about it at this point.

The bell rings, and I look up to see it is 3:15 p.m. I nervously gather my stuff and put it into my book bag. I straighten my desk and take a moment to gain my composure. I walk down the hall, knowing I am going to have to tell Robby in a matter of moments, and I have no idea how or what I am going to say. Jeanna, Robby's sister, and Cara, my best friend since I was three, stopped me in the hall to let me know Robby was here and asked me if we were going to youth tonight. I said yes and thought to myself, *How can I go to church like this?*

I walk to the car and see Robby's face. He is as beautiful and loving as ever. I open the door and slide in first, followed by Jeanna and Cara. Robby touched my leg and looked at me in concern.

"Are you okay?" he asked.

At that moment, I swallowed all the fear down and quietly said, "I am late."

He froze and looked at me and said, "You're late?"

Just then, Jeanna and Cara caught what we were

saying, and the questions started. "How late? When was your last period? Have you been sick? Have you been craving different foods? Have you been peeing a lot?" I was spinning, answering what I could. By the time we got home, we had devised a plan. We would all leave for youth early, and Cara and Jeanna would walk to Walmart from the church and get me a pregnancy test. I was so nervous. Robby did not say much.

Robby dropped me off at my aunt's and took the girls home. I didn't want to talk about it anymore, so I just stewed in my thoughts. I slowly went through the motions of getting ready. The familiar cold feeling had returned. I did not know how I could be a wife or a mother. What was I going to do? I went to the refrigerator and poured me a glass of apple juice. It was cold and crisp. Just as I finished the last sip, I could hear a knock at the door. "Robby and Jeanna and Cara are here," my aunt calls. I slowly walk to the car and wait for the girls to crawl out so I can crawl in. Robby grabs my leg and whispers in my ear, "No matter what, it is going to be okay; please don't worry."

We arrive at the church, I unlock the door, and we pile in one by one. I walk to the front-row seats and just sit there. Robby offers to take the girls to go get the test. He turns toward me and asks if I want to ride. I decline.

Closen But Silenced

He reluctantly turns away and says he will be right back. Robby, Cara, and Jeanna return with a two-pack pregnancy test. I am so nervous; a part of me doesn't want to know. After a few minutes of coaxing by the girls, I finally stand and make my way to the bathroom. I unwrap the test and take the first stick out. I quickly go over the directions so I do not mess it up. I follow the directions to a tee. I wait for the allotted time frame instructed by the instructions. The whole time, they are on the other side of the door, impatiently questioning what I see. I take the stick and the box and compare what I see. I freeze. I walk out to the sanctuary and hand them the test.

Robby impatiently says, "What does it say?"

I whisper, "It says I am pregnant." I visibly see Robby deflate. I straighten my spine and say, "I think it's wrong." So, I walk back into the bathroom and repeat the process.

I come back out a second time and say, "Cara, I need you to go back and get me another two-packer."

"Why?" she asks.

I replied, "Because this one is positive as well, and I think it's probably just a bum pack."

This time, Jeanna and Cara walk to the store, and Robby stays behind with me. He put his arms around me and

128

asked me if I was okay.

I reply, "I am fine, but I know these tests can be wrong, and I am just not convinced."

He looks at me and says, "But you are late."

"I know, but I am cramping, and I read that stress can cause you to be late. I just think this is stress-related, and I am cramping, so I am going to start any day now."

He grabs my chin and says, "You know, if you are pregnant, it's going to be okay, and I can finally marry you." At that moment, a little bit of warmth reached my bones because I knew he wasn't angry about this, and strangely, he may even be a little happy. The girls return with a large drink and two more tests. I grab the test and the drink and proceed to the bathroom. Each time I come out of the bathroom with a positive test, I am convinced they are just defective. Robby and the girls, not so much.

I look at Robby with the last test in my hand, reading positive, and tell him, "I am sure they are all wrong. I will make an appointment at the health clinic for tomorrow, and we will find out for sure." We all take a deep breath and prepare to act as normal as possible for youth group. We grab all the empty pregnancy test boxes and discard them in the Walmart dumpsters by the church. That night, youth group was agonizing. I could not stop thinking about how I might be pregnant and what that means for me. I couldn't help but feel sorry for the baby, if there was one. After all, its mother is a basket case.

I wake up early the next morning. I grab the phone book and the phone and head to the room I am staying in. Thankfully, no one is home, and Aunt Sylvia let me stay home from school today. I make an appointment for 10 a.m., and next, I call Robby. He answers after the first ring. I tell him what time the appointment is, and he lets me know he will be here shortly to pick me up and then hangs up the phone. I pace back and forth in the kitchen until he arrives and run out to his truck the moment I hear him pull up. I slide into the same place I always sit, and we drive in silence all the way there. When Robby pulled into the parking spot, he turned to look at me and asked me if I wanted him to go in with me. I shake my head no. *This is hard enough*, I think to myself.

I slowly walk inside and sign my name on the paper at the front desk where the nurse is sitting. I have no idea what I am doing. My mother always does the paperwork. Someone calls my name, and I am startled and jump up. She said, "Lindsy, I am going to need you to fill out these forms and bring them back to me, and someone will call you back shortly." As I go to turn away, she stops me and asks, "Honey, are you here alone?" I just shake my head yes. I hand in the papers as instructed and wait for my name to be called. It feels like the longest agonizing wait of my life. Then, suddenly, a door swings open, and the nurse calls my name. Everything feels like slow motion; I stand up and take what feels to be the walk of shame toward the nurse. She leads me to the bathroom and instructs me to fill this cup and leave it here and then to sit here. So, I grab the cup from her hand and head to the bathroom to collect my pee. I close the lid, wipe off the cup, and wash my hands. I then place the cup where she has instructed me to and then make my way back to the chair for what feels like another eternity.

The nurse enters the room and sets a chair in close proximity to mine directly across from me. She sits down; she looks serious. She looks at me and says, "Lindsy, do you have anyone here with you?" I shake my head yes and tell her my boyfriend is outside somewhere. She takes a deep breath and says, "Well, I need to tell you that you are pregnant, and I am going to need to take some blood from you." I know I am white as a ghost; I can feel the blood drain from my face. I can see the concern in the nurse's eyes. Everything is spinning, and she is supporting me, asking if I am okay. I could not seem to make out what she was saying right at first. I am frozen solid and scared to death. I gain my composure and let her know I am okay. I reach out my arm to offer my blood. The nurse preps my arm and gathers her supplies so she can take what blood she needs; next, we make a new appointment for a month away. I gather my belongings and my paperwork and walk out of the health department, determined not to cry. I walk to the truck, but Robby isn't there. I called out his name, and he jumped down from the huge tree by the truck. He walks toward me with his hands in his pocket, and I can tell he is so very nervous.

I look at him with tears in my eyes and say, "Well, I guess I am pregnant."

He grabs me tight, wrapping his arms around me, and says, "I am so sorry; everything is going to be okay. We will get married, and I will take care of you guys."

I know he means what he says, but I cannot shake the dread creeping up. I just try and smile and assure him I am okay.

As I reflect on that time in my life, I can't help but be grateful that it was Robby and not some other guy that came into my life. Many young girls get pregnant by boys who don't care and don't stick around. But Robby was different, and we were different. We were young, but we were so in love. I didn't know it then, but I would learn soon that I was meant to be a mom and that I would love all my babies fearlessly! It was my life's mission to keep them safe and to never let them feel the pain I have felt in my past. I would shield and protect them from rejection and trauma. They brought a joy to my soul I had not felt in such a long time. They were just what I needed and right on time. I thank God for them every day.

Chapter 16

TELLING THE PARENTS

"He who covers his sins will not prosper, But whoever confesses and forsakes them will have mercy."

—Proverbs 28:13 (NKJV)

Sitting in my room at my Aunt Sylvia and Uncle Kee's house, I contemplate what I am going to do and how I am going to tell my family. The only people who know I am pregnant at this point are Robby, Jeanna, and Cara. Everyone has taken an oath to say nothing until I can tell my sisters and my parents. I am scared my family will be so disappointed in me, and I am struggling with finding the words to say. My mom and dad are out of the country, so I know I have some time to come up with the words to tell them. My sisters are a completely different story. I love them with all that I am and would never want them to hate me. I get up from my room and head toward the kitchen. I am starving, and the morning sickness has finally subsided. I search the cabinet for the ingredients of my favorite comfort food, tuna casserole. I grab the canned tuna, noodles, and cream of mushroom soup from the pantry. Then, I headed over to the refrigerator and grabbed the milk and cheese. I have a huge smile on my face, knowing comfort is on the way. As I place everything on the counter, my aunt walks into the room and asks me if I have something to tell her. I freeze. I am so confused, having no idea how in the world she knows anything. I say nothing. She fills the empty space with, "I know you are pregnant, and now your parents do too." I am still standing there, unable to find the words to say. My mind racing, I wonder what my parents are feeling or thinking, somewhat relieved I didn't have to say the words to them and knowing they would have some time to process it on the way home from England. Sylvia filled the empty air with words. She proceeded to tell me that we were going to make plans to have Robby and his parent over tonight for dinner to tell them as well. She must have seen the fear in my eyes and walked toward me and told me everything was going to be all right and that she would help me and that we would all sit down together.

Feeling defeated and deflated, I told her I needed to call my sisters and let them know. She said that my parents asked that I speak to no one until they returned.

"Why can't I talk to my sisters?" I ask in protest.

"Because your mother doesn't want anyone to steer you in the wrong direction."

I suddenly understand what she is talking about. I tell her I would never get an abortion. There is a knock at the door, and I go toward the door, and it's Robby. I answer the door, and the look on his face will be forever etched in my mind. He looked tired and so worried. I let him in and told him he couldn't stay long. He looks very distraught and doesn't understand why I am being so cold. I tell him everyone knows and that his parents need to come over tonight so we can tell them together. He agrees and then reluctantly goes home.

The phone rings, and my aunt brings me the phone. As I answer the phone, my aunt does not walk away. I say hello. My sister Toby very sternly says, "Are you pregnant?" I grow cold. How does everyone keep finding out? I have told no one. I say yes and ask how does she know. She tells me she can't believe I didn't tell her and she had to find out at a party with my sister Brandi and that a fight ensued in my honor. Toby was hurt; I never meant to hurt her. I profusely apologize and explain to her that I only found out yesterday and that, somehow, everyone found out before I was able to say anything to the people I cared about the most. We ended the conversation on a good note. All is forgiven and right again between my sisters and me.

I head back to my room to sleep. I am so tired, and I am not ready to face Robby's parents. They hate me already. Robby's mom is hard and harsh and intimidating, and Robby's dad told him once that he should just break up with me and get a dog. He said a dog would be better to have around than me because it would listen better, follows orders, and won't talk back. This is going to be awful. I lay my head on the pillow, but sleep never comes. Just thoughts of the unknown and thoughts of my future. Thoughts of the innocent little baby that is growing inside my belly. I have to do what is right. I have to be strong.

I get up and prepare myself for the impossible task at hand, Robby's parents. I head to the kitchen and help my aunt prepare the dinner. She is being so kind to me. I am so grateful for all the kindness I can get. Sonny and Mindy show up, and I feel like I am going to throw up before supper even gets started. Robby sits next to me at the dinner table. And then everyone else finds a place and sits. Dinner is uneventful; I actually cannot recall any of the small talk spoken at the table that night because I didn't hear it. All I could hear was my heartbeat. Sonny and Kee go to the backyard swing with Robby, and the women clear the table and do the dishes. I cannot recall who or how the words were spoken, but what I can remember is sitting in the living room on the couch with everyone staring at me. Sonny was giving a speech, and I didn't hear a word. I just stared at the floor, waiting for Mindy's anger and wrath. It never came. She finally spoke up and said, "I want to hear from Lindsy." I got the nerve to look at her, and she asked again. "What are you feeling?" I didn't speak. She spoke again, but this time with sadness. She said, "I know just how you are feeling; I have been right where you are, and you are scared to death." Right then, the dam broke, and the tears poured out. She hugged me and said, "I know you are scared, but it's going to be okay; we are all going to be by your side and help you in any way we can." I didn't know till that moment just how overwhelmed I felt. I was unable to process my emotions until then. The crying was a cleansing and just what I needed.

At the time, life was so confusing and so scary, but God! God was always in control. He never left my side. He prepared the way and softened hearts before I even knew I was pregnant. I did not know that when my parents were flying to England, my father had told my mother, "Debra, Lindsy is pregnant." He told her that God had told him. So, before anyone told my parents, the Lord told them. He softened the blow with His own words. I also later found out that when Mindy was cleaning the house, God also told her I was pregnant. I feel like that is why, instead of rage and accusations, I was met with love and understanding.

I do not condone sex before marriage. I am just telling you of the story that led me to a life of redemption and forgiveness. However, I am so glad that I was given such a beautiful gift in a time of utter darkness; I will always be eternally grateful for the beautiful little baby girl God blessed me with at that time in my life. Abortion was never an option for me as I was a survivor of abortion and knew that it was not the answer for me. But life and love were the answer for me. Even if I could not understand or articulate it at the time. That would come much later in life.

Chapter 17

DECEMBER 1995

"Therefore a man shall leave his father and mother and be joined to his wife, and they shall become one flesh."

—**Genesis 2:24 (NKJV)**

I am waiting by the phone impatiently, willing it to ring.

My mom walks into the room and says, "Hey, what are you doing?"

I say, "Ugh, waiting for Robby to call; I know he is home by now!" I am angry and hormonal.

My mom smiles and says, "Just relax; he will call; give the guy a break," and then quietly walks back to her room.

Finally, the phone is ringing. I jerk the phone up to my ear and irritatingly shout hello.

Robby's nervous voice replies, "Hello?"

"Where are you, and why haven't you called?" I shout.

He offensively replies, "I just got home, and I had to take a shower."

"You always come straight here: what is going on? What are you up to?"

"Nothing, I promise. I have a few things to do, and then I am coming over."

"What?" I interject loudly. "What do you mean 'a few things'? I want you to come over right now."

With his voice shaking, he says, "I can't right this second, but I will be over shortly."

I am livid at this point. "Robby, what are you doing? Something isn't right. You would already be over here on a normal day. You are acting strange and hiding something."

And out of fear of my retaliation, he finally concedes. "I am on my way to the jewelry store with Bonnie to get you a ring."

A ring? Oh, what have I done? I have ruined the surprise. God, Lindsy, you are an idiot, I think to myself.

"Wait, why did you tell me? You could have lied."

"No, I couldn't," he replied.

I said, "Okay, I am sorry."

He sighed a deep breath and said, "It's okay."

He asked if I was okay now, and I lied. I said I was fine and I would see him when he came over. We hung up, and I sat in defeat. What was wrong with me? Why was I so untrusting, so scared, and so angry all the time? I just sat there defeated and waiting for him to arrive.

I can see the lights of the truck as he pulls into the drive; I jump up and race out to see him. The way I love this man scares me to death.

I hop in his truck, and I say, "Hey, how you doing?"

He hands me the ring box and says, "Here, you already said you would marry me, and you already know about the ring."

With excitement, I opened the ring box and took out the ring. It was simple and plain, but I loved it, and it was all mine. There was a deep feeling of regret that he didn't propose the way I had always dreamed, but I had no one but myself to blame for that. I am sure I could punish myself for a long time for this. I shove those feelings deep down inside and look up at Robby and give him a big flashing smile and say, "Let's go show my parents."

The next ten days flew by so fast. My mother and father took me to the courthouse to get a marriage license, and it turns out that in the state of Florida, even with your parents' consent, you cannot get married at the age of fifteen. So, my parents and I packed our bags and headed to South Carolina with Robby and his parents. To our dismay, Colleton County refused to give us a marriage certificate as well. As we sat there pondering what the next move was, Mindy called her mother, and it just so happened that she knew the judge in the neighboring town. So, to Manning, South Carolina, we went. December 8, 1995, eight days after I was given a ring, I was married. However, we did not spend the night together that night even though it was heavily protested by Robby. I wanted to wait for a church wedding first; insert deep sigh here.

Two days later, on December 10, 1995, we were married in my parents' church. It was thrown together quickly, but it was amazing. I got to wear my mother's dress, which I had always wanted to do since I was a little girl. My little sister Sheena got to be there. My biological father walked me down the aisle, and the man who raised me performed the ceremony. It was beautiful in its own imperfect way. I was surrounded by the people I loved.

We had a small reception afterward, with cake and presents. People gifted us with so much money. I felt awkward and undeserving of the gifts, but I made it through and just smiled the whole time so no one would know I was so uncomfortable. Once we were done, we gathered all of our belongings and headed for the truck. It was trashed thanks to Robby's friend Scott and his sister Jeanna and my best friend, Cara. We ran through a rain of rice and jumped in the shaving-cream-infested truck. It was everywhere. We shut the doors, we were finally alone, and I was scared to death but happy. After discussing what we wanted to do, we headed for the hotel.

Once we arrived at the hotel, I stayed in the truck while Robby went to get the room. Left alone and to my own thoughts, I was terrified that I was going to go to sleep with this man and wake up with him too. The unknown newness of it was very overwhelming. Then, all of a sudden, Robby comes out of the building, putting his driver's license back in his pocket and frowning. As he opens his side door, I ask what's wrong.

He said, "They say I am not old enough to rent a hotel even if I am married."

I laughed so hard, not realizing seventeen is not old enough to rent a hotel room.

He looks at me, shocked, and then smirks and says, "Shut up, it's not funny; it's embarrassing."

I look him in the eyes and shrug my shoulder and say, "Who cares? Just go back to the church and ask my daddy to come rent the room for us." And, so he did, begrudgingly and sulking all the way there.

My daddy handed Robby the key and hugged me goodnight. I felt so awkward, and maybe even a little shameful, that my dad knew what was going to go down that night. I know it wasn't the first time. But it was the first time I knew that he would know. My emotions were everywhere. I blame the pregnancy. We entered the room, and I sat on the bed.

Robby said, "You feeling okay?"

I said, "Now I am exhausted; it has been a very overwhelming day."

He hung his head and said, "I bet. Let's get your pajamas on and put you to bed."

And so I did. Robby put me to bed, tucked me in, and snuggled up next to me. Not asking for anything but giving me everything I needed. As I drifted off to sleep, I could feel just how lucky I was.

The following morning, as I opened my eyes, I could see a large glass bottle of orange juice. I sat up, and as my eyes cleared, I could see that the table in our room was full of food.

I looked up at Robby and asked, "What is this?"

He said, "Thought you might be hungry, but I didn't know what to get, so I got one of everything off the menu."

At that moment, I was elated with joy, love, and happiness. He was showing me he cared through my love language. Food! We sat and ate and talked about life and what we were going to do, our fears and our hopes. It is one of my most favorite memories of us of all time. It was so simple, but it was pure and real. I fell in love with him a little more; he was so gentle, loving, and patient with me.

"Love suffers long and is kind; love does not envy; love does not parade itself, is not puffed up; does not behave rudely, does not seek its own, is not provoked, thinks no evil; does not rejoice in iniquity, but rejoices in the truth; bears all things, believes all things, hopes all things, endures all things" (1 Corinthians 13:4–7, NKJV).

Chapter 18

WHAT I NEEDED

"And God will wipe away every tear from their eyes; there shall be no more death, nor sorrow, nor crying. There shall be no more pain, for the former things have passed away."

—Revelation 21:4 (NKJV)

I was so broken and confused. I had pushed so many feelings down deep for so long that I had become so bitter, angry, and untrusting. The sad thing is, I was not aware of my behavior completely. The way I reacted or responded to situations I felt were justified. It wasn't until later in life I realized just how miserable I made the people I love feel. My husband, especially, was an easy target; after all, he would just take whatever I dished out and always had.

I did not know what the future held, but I could guess if I looked at my past. I was always waiting for the next thing. Trying to cut it off before it reached me. I behaved poorly in an effort to avoid my own pain, in turn causing pain to the people around me. It was the only way I knew to be. I did not know how to let go and forgive, and I am not sure I even wanted to.

But God loved me; He was fighting for me even though I couldn't see it. Along my journey, He kept giving me nuggets of hope and little treasures to help me through the dark times, knowing that one day I would be able to forgive and let go and let God. Little treasures like my grandparents on both sides, my mom, Arthur, my beautiful sisters, Robby, and my precious children. They are the hope that kept me afloat. What a beautiful gift from God. I would later come to understand through these gifts and to appreciate them. But not at first; many tests and trials would come. God had to take me around the mountain a lot of times before I finally broke and ran to Him.

When I was pregnant with Brianna, my first child, I went to church one night and was called to the front with Robby. There was a song of the Lord that Linda, the praise and worship leader, wanted to sing over us. I cannot remember it all, but it went something like this: "Brianna, I have chosen you, I have chosen you. Since before your birth, I held you and my hand and etched your face. I have called you, I have called you, I have called you. Daddy, tests will come, and through these tests, you will see I am the faithful one. Momma, tears will fall; I will hold you through them all; I will see them as beautiful jewels. I have clothed you in the garments of your gifting; now find your release, find your release." There was so much more to the song, but I can't seem to remember all the words anymore. It was so anointed, I just wept. God was giving me another nugget I didn't know I needed. I have held on to these words throughout the years, even in my darkest hours.

Chapter 19

1996: THE MOVE

"I will bring the blind by a way they did not know; I will lead them in paths they have not known. I will make darkness light before them, And crooked places straight. These things I will do for them, And not forsake them."

—Isaiah 42:16 (NKJV)

Placing the last box in the back of the truck, I turn and look at the one-room apartment attached to Robby's parents' house that I have called home for the last several months. I take a deep breath and try and push down the sadness deep in my soul. I know this is the right thing to do. It is cheaper to live in South Carolina; it is where Robby was raised. He promises he can give us a better life there. I do love adventure and new places, I remind myself, and this is the natural way of things. He did promise we could come back if I didn't like it. But, still, there is a void in my heart. I will miss my sisters, my parents, and my friends. I am only fifteen, and the thought of moving so far away from my parents is gut-wrenching. But I am going to do what is right and follow my husband wherever he takes us. I hug my parents one last time, careful not to cry. I look in my rearview mirror as we pull away; I can see my mother weeping as my father holds her. Warm salt streams roll down my cheeks. I know I have to be strong; I am just tired of being strong. We are going to stay with Robby's sister, and I am grateful, but she doesn't even like me; she is very cold toward me. I know I deserve it, but do I really have to endure this? I feel like my heart is ripping in two. I look up, and Robby is looking at me with concern; wiping my tears away, he gives me a crooked smile and says, "Hey, it's going to be okay; we will come back and visit all the time." Drying my eyes, I try and focus on more positive things. What will it be like? Will I make new friends? Will we find our own place? My spirits lift a little, but not completely, as we travel the six and a half hours to our new town.

Pulling off ramp 57 into Walterboro, South Carolina, I am hopeful, maybe, just maybe, life will be great here. I am nervous and apprehensive of the unknown, but I am positive as long as I am with Robby and Brianna, everything will be okay. We pull into Bonnie's drive, and she is waiting for us. I see Taylor, my niece, and my face lights up, a playmate for Brianna. We get out of the car. As I am getting

Brianna from her car seat, Bonnie affectionately gives her brother a hug. Then, graciously but coldly, she offered me a hug. *Great, already off to a good start!* I think. She hates me, and I have to live here. My insides are screaming; I want to go home where I am loved, valued, and cherished. I push that down and proceed into the house.

Let me just say I will forever be eternally grateful; Bonnie opened her house up to us and took us in and helped us start our new life. I am just trying to paint a picture of what I was feeling in my new land. Almost immediately, I knew I hated the Walterboro–Ruffin area. Everything was different. I was not easily accepted by Robby's family and friends. I am not sure if it was just me they didn't like or the fact they thought I trapped Robby into a loveless relationship. What I do know is that it was extremely emotionally hard for me to move states away from my family, where I was loved, to a place where no one liked me. I am not saying I was easy to love because, believe me, I know now I was almost impossible to love. I am just saying I did not adjust well. However, for Robby, it was like he never left in the first place. He was thriving and so happy. A few months after we moved there, I begged Robby to take me home. I reminded him he said if I didn't like it, we could go home. He simply laughed and said, "We are here now; we are not going anywhere." He assured me

I would adapt eventually. When he left that day for work, I remember just crying myself to sleep, feeling so hopeless. I felt trapped and like I was lied to, and I was. This only added another layer to my scared soul. The bitterness was festering under the surface, and I was not even aware it would eventually wreak havoc on my body many years down the road on my journey.

Chapter 20

DEAL WITH IT NOW

"Finally, brethren, whatever things are true, whatever things are noble, whatever things are just, whatever things are pure, whatever things are lovely, whatever things are of good report, if there is any virtue and if there is anything praiseworthy—meditate on these things. The things which you learned and received and heard and saw in me, these do, and the God of peace will be with you."

—Philippians 4:8–9 (NKJV)

No matter what you have gone through in your life, it is imperative you deal with it the moment you are able. The longer you allow bitterness, anger, resentment, and unforgiveness to take root, the worse it will become. It will grow like a disease to your soul and will even affect your physical body. Whether the offense is large or small, it doesn't matter. Take it to the Lord, pray. If you are able to communicate with the person causing your pain, then have the hard talks. It's never too late to let it go and let God!

Remember, you may be a source of the offenses spoken to someone else. Take the time to evaluate your past and offer an apology to the ones you have hurt so their healing can begin. In the end, it is not about who is wrong or right. It is about redemption and relationship with the Father in heaven. He longs for all of His children to be redeemed and to walk with Him.

The most important thing to do is pray. Start by praying for the ones who have hurt you, the ones who have persecuted you. Even if you don't know the words to pray, start simple. Release them from whatever offense you hold them to, and pray for salvation of their souls. We are all God's children, and the one thing we as human beings have in common is we all want to be loved and accepted. He wants us, and He accepts us. So, remember that as you pray for your brothers and sisters who are lost. Many people may hurt you and not even know it, including you. The truth is, hurt people hurt people, and until you recognize your own hidden pain, you will never realize the pain you are inflicting on others. Remember, the greatest commandment is love.

Chapter 21

1995-2004: THE QUIET YEARS

To everything there is a season, A time for every purpose under heaven: A time to be born, And a time to die; A time to plant, And a time to pluck what is planted; A time to kill, And a time to heal; A time to break down, And a time to build up; A time to weep, And a time to laugh; A time to mourn, And a time to dance; a time to cast away stones, And a time to gather stones; A time to embrace, And a time to refrain from embracing; A time to gain, And a time to lose; A time to keep, And a time to throw away; A time to tear, And a time to sew; A time to keep silence, And a time to speak; A time to love, And a time to hate; A time of war, And a time of peace.

—Ecclesiastes 3:1–8 (NKJV)

These years of my life had their challenges, being a new wife and mother and in a new place surrounded by strangers, as you could probably imagine. I was fifteen and newly married with a baby on the way. I had no idea how to be a mother or a wife, but I took on this next part of my life with excitement. I always wanted to love and be loved. I had so much hope and so many expectations for my future. I did not know just how challenging it would be; my view on love was very distorted, and I was starting this family with a very broken soul.

I was so young and naive; everything that Robby did or said would hurt me and cut me so deep the man didn't stand a chance. The more he tried, the harder I would push away. I was not a good wife or even a good friend. He was young and loved to hang out with his friends. He would work all day and then go hunting and fishing in his free time. The more I got left alone, the more resentful I became. I was so angry that he moved me so far away from my family, only to leave me all alone. This is one of the many issues our marriage faced.

The first to arrive in our little family was Brianna Lea Cummings on May 14, 1995, after only three pushes and seven hours and fifty-four minutes of labor. She was so beautiful and perfect in every way. She was born bald with the most beautiful piercing blue eyes and her tiny little mouth and nose. She weighed six pounds and seven ounces. As she grew, her personality started to shine through; she was headstrong, intelligent, and so loving. Every morning, she would wake up, go to the refrigerator, get her bottle on the bottom shelf, and then head to the living room, dragging her beanbag behind her. Then she would get a Barney VHS tape and put it in the VCR and watch Barney until I would wake up, all at the tender age of one year old. She was potty-trained way before her second birthday. She brought so much joy and happiness into my life; a life that was so lonely was now filled with a precious life of laughter and companionship I was needing so much. I spent my days playing hide-and-seek and watching Barney. For the first time, the darker time of my life faded into the background, and a resemblance of peace began to fill the forefront, even if it was only for a little while.

Next to arrive in our little clan was Ethan Gabriel Cummings on March 4, 2000, after one good push and three hours of labor. He was long and skinny and the biggest baby I ever had, weighing a whopping seven pounds twelve ounces. He was so sweet, quiet in nature, and soft-spoken. He was a little slower to be potty-trained, and he relied on me for everything, unlike his sister. I truly loved it! I loved being needed. I loved being loved. He would love to crawl into my lap and snuggle randomly, and I ate it up. The other side of him was all boy; he loved the outside and playing in the dirt. He wanted to be just like his daddy in every sense of the word. As he got older, he got the nickname Eeyore because he always was so quiet and humdrum at times. He was just what I needed. He would make me smile every time he came into the room, and Brianna loved having a baby around; what a good big sister. With the birth of my second child, my peace grew even more.

The final member to arrive, or so we thought, was Malaki Owen Cummings, born May 27, 2002, after one and a half hours of labor and the doctors telling me not to push, but it didn't matter; he came flying out all by himself. He weighed six pounds, even with gorgeous blue eyes and blond hair. Malaki came into this world surrounded by drama. He was born breathing super fast and not transitioning well and had to spend a few days in the NICU. He had a spinal tap and was tube-fed. I was so sad, and so worried, they wouldn't let me nurse him at first. I wouldn't leave the hospital. As he grew up, he continued to attract attention. He would dance around the house doing the diaper dance and would always try to make the family laugh. He was my silly goofball and fiercely independent. He was loud, always singing and causing drama. He loved getting all the attention. I just knew he would be famous one day. My children kept me on my toes and entertained me, which was the distraction I needed to keep my mind off all the disappointments I felt in my very lonely marriage.

I can remember that during a lot of these years, I would constantly have praise and worship music playing in my house; my favorite was *Hope* by Hillsong. It set an atmosphere of peace, which I craved constantly. I had very few friends, and from time to time, I would slip away and hang out with what friends I had, but when I felt the darkness creeping up and fear and anxiety trying to take back over, I would start playing my music again. I didn't realize it then, but setting the atmosphere in my home of peace with praise and worship and the love of my children is what kept me from going under and giving up completely.

During this time in my life, my little sister Sheena often came to stay with us during the summers a few times; she also came from a broken home and a broken past. So, I always wanted her around so I could love on her and guide her, protect her, and help her through. We were able to get her off her ADHD medications, and she just fit perfectly with the rest of us. She would later come to live with us and start her very own relationship with the Lord, but I will tell you more about that later on.

This time in my life wasn't without issues, as I was newly married, with kids, a sister, living in a new place and on family land. I had so many fights with my in-laws.

So even though this time in my life is considered quiet because there were no sexual attacks, it was not all roses; remember, I had a lot of anger and bitterness, and I fought anyone who wasn't in the new family I had started or my family back home. And the truth of the matter is, I just didn't get along with Robby's family at all; they hated me, and for good reason, and the feelings were mutual. It wasn't until a few years ago that God started to really heal and restore the relationship I have with his parents. I didn't stop to think for a second that they had their own issues and struggles they were going through and that it could be why they treated me the way they did. Everyone has a story, and hurt people hurt people.

There isn't much in this life that I am proud of, but I can say with all honesty I am so proud to be the mother to my four children. Yes, I said four, but the fourth one doesn't come till much later. If I never do anything else in my life, I am so happy that God chose me to be their mother! What a gift, what a treasure they have been to me. I failed in so many areas in my life, but I never wanted anything more in this life than to be a good mother and for my children to know they are loved! I would do anything for my children, and I thank God for them every single day.

Chapter 22

2004: THE FIFTH ATTEMPT

"He who dwells in the secret place of the Most High Shall abide under the shadow of the Almighty. I will say of the Lord, 'He is my refuge and my fortress; My God, in Him I will trust.' Surely He shall deliver you from the snare of the fowler And from the perilous pestilence. He shall cover you with His feathers, And under His wings you shall take refuge; His truth shall be your shield and buckler. You shall not be afraid of the terror by night, Nor of the arrow that flies by day, Nor of the pestilence that walks in darkness, Nor of the destruction that lays waste at noonday. A thousand may fall at your side, And ten thousand at your right hand; But it shall not come near you. Only with your eyes shall you look, And see the reward of the wicked. Because you have made the Lord, who is my refuge, Even the Most High, your dwelling place, No evil shall befall you, Nor shall any plague come near your dwelling; For He shall give His angels charge over you, To keep you in all your ways. In their hands

they shall bear you up, Lest you dash your foot against
a stone. You shall tread upon the lion and the cobra, The
young lion and the serpent you shall trample underfoot.
    'Because he has set his love upon Me, therefore I will
deliver him; I will set him on high, because he has known
My name. He shall call upon me, and I will answer him;
I will be with him in trouble; I will deliver him and honor
him. With long life I will satisfy him, And show him My
salvation.'"

—Psalm 91:1–16 (NKJV)

Laughing, I hit send, replying to my best friend's question she had asked me just moments before on my IM. The house is so quiet. Robby and the kids just left for church at the tabernacle in the front of our property. I bailed on them tonight again; I am feeling so tired and just want some peace and quiet, time alone, no one asking for me to do something, no one to scream "Mom," just some boring old silence.

I walk into the kitchen and rummage through the cabinets, looking for a snack. I find chips, crackers, soups, and some stuff I could cook, but I am feeling super lazy. I grab the bag of chips and a soda from the fridge and head back to my computer to finish chatting with my friend. I am feeling relaxed and silly, smiling at my next reply. I type a quick message, giggle, and hit send again. I open my bag of chips and put a few in my mouth, savoring the cheesy flavor saturating my tongue, and chase it down with a swallow of soda.

I look out the window and take notice of how dark it has gotten in such a short time. I am sitting there waiting for my friend to reply when all of a sudden, I see lights pull up in my front yard quickly and in the spot Robby always parks. I quickly tell my friend I have to go because Robby's home and must need me for something. As I am shutting down the computer, he walks through the bedroom door and starts quickly kissing me. It happens so fast and so abruptly that it takes me a second before I realize this isn't Robby. I am confused; my alarms are going off incessantly, and all of my past is flooding back. I cannot hear anything; everything is fuzzy; I can't see very well as panic starts to set in. The only thought going through my head at this time is, *Not again, please not again.*

I somehow get far enough away from this man I know very well, and I say I have to use the bathroom. He says, "Okay." I walk very quickly to my room, everything still fussy, I cannot seem to get enough air, and my vision is narrowing. I grab the phone off my bed and go to the bathroom and sit on the toilet. I try and make my hands work to dial, but my thoughts are not working. Just then, there he is in my bathroom; he grabs the phone and tosses it into my bedroom. I get up and pull my pants up. I force a smile and a nervous laugh. I walk through the other door to try and get away from him. Once through the door, I start running. I make it out the front door to my front yard. I can hear my husband playing music just yards away; I let out the loudest scream I have ever screamed. I can feel his arms grip me from behind, and he puts his hand over my mouth and tells me to be quiet. His voice has an eerie cold sound to it.

I completely shut down. I am now in survival mode. I have been here before, I survived, and I made it to today. I am taken to his truck, where I am flipped around and raped from behind. I can still hear my husband playing music and singing. My mind is focused on Robby's sound; I am fading away, I am cold, I am empty. He releases me, and as he is putting himself back together, I quickly walk to my door; I turn to see if he is going to leave, and he is smiling; he says, "Hey, we are both Aries, and we are impulsive," as to justify what he has just done to me.

I go inside and lock all the doors. I slowly sink to the couch; I cannot feel anything; I am so numb; I am so cold. After what seems to be an eternity of blankness, I get up from the couch and walk to the bathroom. I turn the shower on as hot as it will go. Maybe I can warm myself up and stop this shaking. I step into the shower and let the scolding water wash away the filth from my body; the shivering stops, but the numbness doesn't leave. Why can't I feel? Why am I not crying? I get my clothes on and walk back to the living room and turn on a movie. Slowly, the color returns to my face, and I am able to concentrate somewhat on the movie.

There is a knock at the front door, and my heart skips a beat until I hear the sound of my children coming through the door. My heart thaws at the sound of my family returning home. I open the door and smile, genuinely happy they are home. I look at my husband to see if he can tell that I am different, but he just smiles and heads to the kitchen. I do not know how, but I am able to collect my kids and perform my regular mother tasks. I am so grateful that no one knows and that I am able to function even though all my feelings are gone.

That was one of the worst times in my life; I did not realize then the damage that night would have on me for years to come. I was forever changed. I cannot say if it was this trauma alone or the combination of past events and the new trauma that made the most impact. What I can say is that with each event, I was fractured a little at a time; the multiple fracturing left me little of myself to hold onto. That night, the piece of me that broke away was too large for me to bear. I was shattered, and I no longer had the ability to trust, feel, or care. This person was someone I knew well. Someone who was married with kids and a friend of the family. How could a father, a husband, and a friend do something like this and not even bat an eye? Clearly, no one can be trusted; there have just been too many attacks. No one is good; everyone is bad. This was the start of my self-destruction and the plan of the enemy all along.

Chapter 23

HARVEST TIME

"For I know the thoughts that I think toward you, says the Lord, thoughts of peace and not of evil, to give you a future and a hope."

—Jeremiah 29:11 (NKJV)

At this point in my life, I am angry, bitter, and broken. I trust no one and hate everyone. I am physically fighting with my in-laws, and I cannot get along with anyone. I have just recently got into another altercation with my mother-in-law, and my husband is staying neutral. So, I packed up my things, along with my kids, and rented an apartment in town. It isn't long before Robby shows up at my door and joins me in the city. I can't look at him anymore the way I used to. I blame him for everything. I blame him for moving me away from my family, I blame him for his family mistreating me, and I blame him for the rape. I cannot even listen to him play music without becoming sick. But I get up every day, paint a smile on my face, and walk numbly through life.

It is during this time that Robby starts going to a church called Harvestime. I can see he is trying to save our marriage, but I just don't believe him; I am waiting for him to go back to the Robby that must be in Ruffin, hunting and fishing and always leaving me all alone. He asked me to go to church one night, and I reluctantly complied. I walk through the doors in my ripped jeans and sit somewhere in the middle of the left-side column. I do not want to make eye contact with anyone, and Robby is talking to everyone. The service begins, and I am good for the first couple of songs, and then all of a sudden, Toni, the pastor's wife, starts to sing a song, and the anointing becomes so thick, I feel a warm tear roll down my cheek. Confused, I wipe it away. That is when I noticed the pain I was feeling in my chest; it was tight and very unwelcome. I have been able to go this long not feeling, and I didn't realize just how much I really didn't want to feel. I was in protection mode, and now, in this moment, I was unable to keep the shield up; the presence of God was penetrating through it all.

I didn't know what I was walking into when I said yes that night, but God did. Over the course of several years, God began to heal my marriage using Pastor Darrel and Toni. I began to pray more and to worship again. I went through many nights of counseling. It was through one of these counseling sessions that Darrel said, "Lindsy, if you want your marriage to work, you cannot have any more secrets." So, Robby and I pour out our truths to one another with them by our sides. That is the night Robby found out about all the terrible things that had happened to me, including the most recent and all the terrible things I had done. I thought for sure my life would be over and that I would end up alone if I ever spoke these things out for anyone to hear. The funny thing is, the complete opposite happened. I had a feeling of freedom I had never felt before, and I was at peace.

It was through this time I started to learn about forgiveness; I watched my husband, broken from my past, having a hard time dealing with all the truths, struggling, as I was just overwhelmed with joy I could feel again. I didn't know if we would make it, but I knew I was feeling and on the path to loving and trusting again, and maybe, just maybe, I would be able to forgive. I woke up one night in my bed alone. I got up to look for Robby, and he was in the living room, kneeling on the couch, weeping. I carefully approached him and placed my hand on his shoulder; he turned and looked at me. I asked him if he was okay, and he said yes. He embraced me and said, "I forgive you; I love you so much." He began to tell of the things God was showing him about forgiveness and how God was healing his heart. I was amazed. I thought, *How is this possible?* I wanted to feel that too. I wanted to heal; I wanted to trust; I wanted to love; I wanted to not be afraid all the time.

Even though I was healing, it was a slow process for me, but as I watched the true transformation of my husband, it helped me to believe and to seek out that which he had found. I would not find it for years to come. But this was the beginning of my healing, of *our* healing. We did eventually move back to our country home in Ruffin, but things were different this time. They were better. We were firmly planted in a church and surrounded by godly people who loved us. I was often triggered by my surroundings as my house and yard were a source of pain, but with our new life, I was able to cope and work on a better me.

I will never forget the time I spent at Harvestime Ministries and the people who poured their hearts and souls into our lives. It is ministries like this and people who are willing to answer the call that make it possible for the unreachable to be reached. Everyone needs someone at some point in their lives to love them unconditionally, to help guide them, hold their hand if needed, and lead them to the Father, where the true healings come from. I was blessed enough to have that through them.

Chapter 24

THE PERFECT GIFT

"Behold, children are a heritage from the Lord, The fruit of the womb is a reward."

—Psalm 127:3 (NKJV)

The kids are sitting on the couch watching cartoons, and the house is finally quiet as a house with three kids can be when the phone rings. I run to pick it up, and it is my little sister Sheena on the other line. She is frantic. She is saying she is pregnant and if I don't go get her before the next morning, she is having an abortion; the appointment is already made. I close my eyes, and I think, *It is late afternoon, and she lives seven hours away; what am I going to do?* I start walking to my bedroom, trying to not let anyone hear our conversation; I hear the Lord tell me, "Lindsy, you were saved for such a time as this." I think, *Well, you better tell my husband because he isn't gonna let me go.* And I hear it again, but this time with more urgency. "You were born for such a time as this." So, I tell my sister that everything is going to be okay but that I need to call her back. I hang up and call Robby immediately. I tell him about the call from Sheena, and then I tell him what I felt like the Lord had said. He replies almost instantly, "Well, then you have to go, but you can't go alone; see if someone will ride with you." I thank him and hang up. I sit there and think, *Who can I call? Who will stop what they are doing and leave late in the day to drive all night to Florida?* I didn't have to think very hard; I knew one fun-loving, free-spirited, spontaneous person who would do anything for their friends, and her name was Tiffany! I call her immediately, tell her what is happening, and ask if she would ride with me, and without hesitation, she says, "Yes, just give me an hour, and I will be ready." I thank her, hang up the phone, and squeal with excitement. I run quickly to my room, throw my stuff in a bag, and then rush to the kitchen to make sure there is food for my family to eat tonight. Just as I am about to be ready to leave, Robby arrives and takes over; pressing a kiss on my mouth, he whispers, "I love you, and be safe. I will take care of everything here until you get back."

Tiffany and I had been driving for hours, laughing and cutting up, and then we would get serious and talk about the deeper, heavy stuff and then back to laughing when the phone rang. I answer it, and it is Sheena, and she is crying hysterically; I can't even make out what she is saying to me. After getting her to breathe and calm down, that's when she told me she was just jumped by a group of people, boys and girls. One of the boys that was fighting her was the father of the baby. He had brought the group over to jump her in hopes of killing the baby. I tell her to go inside, lock the door, and I will be there in thirty minutes. I was so close, but so far, all I wanted was to protect my sister and the baby in her womb and beat up the people who were trying to hurt them; I was raging. I hang up the phone, and Tiffany prays with me, and the anger subsides. We pray for protection over her and that God would bring her peace and comfort during this time.

We finally arrive and get Sheena into the car and start to head back to South Carolina. I was not prepared for the Sheena that entered my car that day; I hadn't been with her for a couple of years, and she had changed so much. She pulls out some cigarettes and tries to light one up, and I throw them out the window. So when we stop at the next rest stop, she walks over to a man at a pay phone and asks if she can please bum a cigarette. I see her and realize what she is doing, and I beeline for them. As the man is getting a cigarette for my sister, I yell, "Don't you dare give her a cigarette; she is underage and pregnant, and I will call the law." I laugh at the thought of it now. That man was probably like, "I don't want anything to do with you, crazy people." Because after I yell at him, he walks off in the other direction.

She turns to me and says, "I can't believe you won't let me have a cigarette."

I say, "Well, you're pregnant, and it's bad for you, and if you are staying with me, there will be no smoking."

She deep sighs and then screams, "But it isn't fair," turns, and walks back to the car. She didn't have much to say the rest of the trip.

We arrive in Ruffin, and Sheena has a huge chip on her shoulder, but she smiles when she sees her niece and nephews and brother-in-law. I am not going to lie and say it was all peaches and cream because it wasn't. She was a broken teenager with issues, and I was a broken adult with issues, but we loved each other fiercely. Our only requirements of her were no cussing, no long-distance phone calls, no smoking, and she had to go to church, and we didn't bend. In fact, we lived thirty minutes from town on 112 acres and only went to town once a day. So, I let her know that we were ready to go and if she didn't get in the car, she wouldn't be able to go to town and go out to eat with us afterward, and she kept dragging her feet and so we left, and she had to stay home alone. After that, she never missed a service. She grew to love our church family as much as we did. I noticed a real change in her attitude and relationship with the Father, and her bump was ever-growing.

She let us know that she could not take care of the baby; she wasn't able due to her life circumstances. We just kept talking baby names with her in hopes that she would change her mind once the baby was born, but she had an anchor back home, and home kept calling to her even though there was nothing good for her there except our dad. So, after much discussion, she finally picks out a name, Isaiah Moshay Taylor. We are so excited at this point. Baby due any day, name picked out, Sheena has finally gotten a relationship with the Lord and some much-needed inner healing. But we don't know what's going to happen after this baby arrives, but we don't care; we just know he was meant to be alive!

The day arrives, and Sheena delivers Isaiah three weeks early. He is so tiny, with the most beautiful color skin that most mixed babies have, a head full of dark curly brown hair, dark brown eyes, and a bruise across his little square-shaped nose. He is perfect in every way. They bond immediately; she holds him and looks into his eyes and weeps as she reads him a letter she prepared for just this occasion. Everyone in the room cried. It was truly a beautiful moment, and you could tell how much love she had for him in that moment.

At her six-week checkup, she got the all clear. She comes to Robby and me and tells us that she is going home and leaving Isaiah here with us; she had been saying that the whole time she had been pregnant, but we never thought she would actually go through with it, especially after seeing how loving and motherly she always was with him. However, we were wrong; she had a letter written out giving us custody, not legally, but it was something. I helped her gather her stuff, and she went back home to Florida. After that, I was torn between two emotions: the sadness from the loss of my sister, whom I had grown so close to over the past eight months, and the happiness I felt from the addition of a new baby in our home.

Isaiah Moshay Cummings, what a gift from God. He was such an agile little kid, happy, rambunctious, a climber, and loved to hang out on the top of the refrigerator. He brought a newfound joy to our lives and gave us hope for a new beginning. He is so gentle and caring and gets along with everyone. He was always Robby's sidekick, and they are inseparable. After many hard years, we were able to make the adoption final. He adds so much to our lives. I am forever grateful I heard the voice of the Lord and that Isaiah was saved. I couldn't imagine a world without Isaiah in it!

At this point in my life, I felt like nothing else bad could happen and that life was good, at least for a little while. I didn't know it at this point yet, but I am going to learn about loss in the future in a way I could have never imagined, and it would shake everything I have ever known to be true.

Chapter 25

JULY 22, 2009: LOSS

"Blessed are those who mourn, For they shall be comforted."

—Matthew 5:4 (NKJV)

I lay across my father's bed, watching him struggle for each breath; he is unable to respond; he is all bones. My heart is so heavy; I can hear the song "The More I Seek You" on repeat in the background. My thoughts drift: How is this happening? How have we come to this point? This is a man who was diagnosed with an incurable disease years before; he went to the mountains alone and sought hard after God and came home healed, with no traces of the disease to be found. He is a man of great faith; people are healed by the presence of God when he prays for them. So, why am I sitting on this bed watching him waste away, unable to speak and struggling for every breath? I am confused and want God to move, but nothing is changing.

My mother enters the room and gently lies across my

father and whispers in his ears, "It's okay, you can go, we will be okay, I will be okay, you don't have to suffer anymore." In that instance, I go cold, an all-too-familiar feeling. I am numb, and I want to be anywhere but there because I know that this release that she just gave him is all he needed. I know he was fighting for her. I go to him and kneel and kiss his face one last time; I whisper, "I love you." I turn toward my sister Toby, who is crying, and I say I want to go somewhere and get drunk. We leave and head somewhere, anywhere but there. I am now sitting at a table outside, surrounded by my sister Toby's friends; we are all talking and drinking. I feel something, but I am not sure what it is because it's bathed in alcohol. I am not sure how long we have been here, how much we have drank, or what was said. Toby looks at me and says, "Okay, it's time to go."

I walk through my mother's house, into my mother's room. Arthur is there; his respirations have slowed, but he is still struggling for each breath. We all surround him and cry; we know it won't be long now. I am drunk and so overwhelmed with grief. I can hear the worship music playing as he takes his last breath. I fall to the bed and weep. I can hear my mother weeping, and I weep harder. He is gone, just like that. I will never hear his voice; I will never see his smile; he will never toss me in the air again.

I can feel my body shutting down again, no matter how hard I will it to feel. The grief, the anger, and the pain are flooding me, and my body is slipping away into protective mode again.

I dress for the funeral with my family, and we head to the church. This time, instead of seeing his happy, charismatic self hopping around the stage, preaching, there were flowers and a giant picture of him. No open casket; he wouldn't have wanted people to see him that way. Just two huge pictures depicting the essence of who he was, a beautiful man with so much compassion, kind eyes, full of energy, and always smelling of cinnamon due to the fact he loved to suck on Fireballs. This seems so surreal; there are so many people here. But I can't tell you a single name. I am lost in a sea of blankness; I am in a haze. My children are crying; their poppy is gone, but I can't comfort them. I am stuck. Empty.

Robby walks onto the stage and sings a song; it's a song that he wrote for me while he was home and I was taking care of Arthur miles away. I would call so upset. One night after one of these phone calls, he starts to pray, asking God why and how can he help me through this. God replied to Robby with the song he is now singing on the stage. It's called "The Storm." I can't make out the words right now;

I am in and out of it. I look up onto the balcony, and I see Dr. Franado; he took care of Arthur while he was sick; he put his hand over his heart and nodded his head at me. I feel a little of something at that moment, but it passes as quickly as it comes, and I turn my attention back to Robby singing his song. I envy the emotion I see on his face. I am cold again. I just need this nightmare to end.

I cannot tell you in detail everything that happened that day, who rode with who, who was there, how I got to the grave site, or what was even said at either of the services. This was a dark time for me. I know people lose loved ones all the time and are not traumatized. But, it did something to me. It made me question everything I had ever known to be true. Was God real? My dad, a man of great faith who loved God with all of his heart, who never did anything wrong like the people who have hurt me, could die while they lived; then, was any of this even real? I was angry, I was confused, and I was done.

Chapter 26

REFLECTION

"You, who have shown me great and severe troubles,
Shall revive me again, And bring me up again from the
depths of the earth. You shall increase my greatness, And
comfort me on every side."

—Psalm 71:20–21 (NKJV)

From this time until 2016, I stayed in a very dark place. I wanted to give up, but I couldn't because of my beautiful babies and my loving husband, but I didn't know how to process everything that had happened to me in my life up until this point. I was so confused. I didn't even know how I felt about God or if He was even real. Was this all an illusion? Was there any good left in the world? Arthur wasn't a perfect man by any means, but he was perfect for us; he rescued us in a time when we really needed to be rescued. He loved and cared for us, and now he is gone.

I think the combination of the premature death of my father and all the traumas I faced with no one to help me to process all the emotions I was feeling was very detrimental to my emotional and physical health. I was starting to notice frequent bouts of sickness. I didn't realize until much later that the only way I knew how to continue on this life was to compartmentalize each trauma into its own little safe place and lock it down. This doesn't mean that I never thought about them because the intrusive thoughts defiantly flooded me on a continual basis. In time with no one to help me, I turned completely against myself. The self-hate was so deeply rooted, and I didn't even know it was there. I would have fits of rage, days of total seclusion; if my family wanted to spend time with me, they would just have to come crawl into my bed with me. I would have moments of panic attacks and severe depression, and I just didn't know what to do.

At night, I would be shaking and crying in fear, and Robby would have to play his guitar and sing worship songs until I fell asleep. One time, I was home alone, minding my own business, when fear hit me and stopped me dead in my tracks. I was frozen in place and could see my bedroom door in the distance; it was black, and I had this sudden feeling that someone was in there and was going to jump out and hurt me. So, I looked at my phone as my hearing started to get muffled, and I called Robby and said, "I need you now." He was there in a matter of seconds, praying over me and holding me, reassuring me everything was going to be okay. When I think about it, even now, it brings tears to my eyes; how did I not see this precious gift, Robby, that God had placed in my life to help me through some pretty dark times? But I am stubborn, and I needed God to help me out of this pit and show me the way. Robby and I were just not on the same page. He was a good man, but he didn't understand the depths of my trauma or how to help me through it. One of the main issues was one of my traumas actually happened in my front yard, so every time I would pull up to my house, I would have to relive the event. So, when I asked if we could move for the nine hundredth time, it was the same old, "I am never leaving this property; it is my inheritance." My reply would be, "Anything could happen, and your dad could lose his land tomorrow." And in the end, his parents divorced, and nobody is left on the land except for Robby's father. I didn't realize it then, but all I needed was for Robby to put us first and take me away from the place that was a source of so much pain for me. So we stayed, and things got much worse before they got better.

Chapter 27

THE FADE

*"But I fear, lest somehow, as the serpent deceived Eve
by his craftiness, so your minds may be corrupted from
the simplicity that is in Christ."*

—**2 Corinthians 11:3 (NKJV)**

Over the next several years, I started attending church
less and less until I was no longer darkening the doors.
I was attending school to be a registered nurse, pouring
everything into that; all my time and devotion went into
school, and I slipped further and further away from my
family. My anxiety returned with a vengeance. I started
checking locks several times a night, checking the trunk
and back seat of my car before entering it. I would get out
of my car and would hit the key fob lock multiple times
and then would have to leave wherever I was to come
and hit it a few more times to make sure it was locked. As
the compulsion grew more and more ridiculous, I left my
house less and less. I would only leave to attend school

and work. When I was home, I would stay in my room for most of the time. I would only come out for food or when forced.

I was slipping further and further away from my family and losing touch with what was real. I would have full-fledged panic attacks. My life was under siege, and I was drowning. This is when I sought help through a psychiatrist and was put on the max amount of Prozac along with Ativan and Klonopin to cope while I went through cognitive behavioral therapy. At first, I was a zombie, but as the therapy helped me deal and cope, I was slowly weaned off the medications. I graduated from nursing school off of medications and was able to live somewhat of an existence. I was still messed up and confused on the inside, but I had the power to deal with this picture of a life I had painted to a certain degree.

I started working night shifts in the ICU and making the most money I had ever made, and Robby started working selling insurance, making more money than me. Our house was paid off, and our bills were minimal. For the first time ever, we were not struggling or begging for money. I thought this was the answer. Now we can be happy. We started spending more and more time apart; he would take two- to three-week trips, and I would pick up extra shifts in order to cope with being alone. We were pretty much living our own lives doing our own things. This is where I believe we left a door for the enemy to come into an already very broken environment.

It was during this time that I started to form relationships with the people I worked with; we became really close. It's funny how relationships form under stress. I worked around the clock with these individuals and, at times, spent more time with them than I did with my own family. I worked the night shift because I had a tremendous fear of the nighttime. It was easier to sleep during the day when I was alone. Robby was never home, but he was making money, so I decided not to say anything. This is what we needed, so I thought. I was so lonely and so scared, I started to become very bitter instead of discussing the issues with my husband. I became very close to a man I was working with and slipping further and further away from my husband. It was a slow fade. I would have long talks with this guy about my life, my marriage, and my loneliness. Out of my conversations with him, I realized I was not what Robby needed. I began to believe that I was not like Robby and that he was a good man and destined for great things. I was holding him back; I was the poison in his camp. So, I allowed myself to slip further away. I believed that I was never meant for the life I had chosen and that I needed to be with someone like me, someone who wasn't sure of God's existence, someone who watched bad movies and listened to worldly music. Someone I could just be myself around. Someone I wouldn't have to pretend with. To be with someone who accepted me for the broken trash I had become.

At first, before I was too far gone, Robby and I both heard the Father call us to Tennessee, but we didn't go. Robby was content, and in my mind, I knew he would never leave Ruffin and that I would have to live on the property, constantly being triggered and living in fear. Robby stopped doing ministry, bought a boat, and said, "I know God called us to Tennessee, but I am going to stay right here. We will be fine." It was in that instant that he said he felt God remove His hand and that he was all alone.

At some point, I don't recall when, I must have ordered *The Story of Us* by the Beavers in a last-ditch effort to save my marriage. Because on the day I called Robby and told him I was leaving to be with someone else and that I couldn't be with him anymore, he said, "You got a package in today, and can I bring it to you and talk for a minute?" I agreed; I felt he deserved at least that much. As I approached the vehicle, he handed me the package; it was the teaching I had ordered, and I froze. Because on the front of the book was a tree trunk with its ring. This was so significant to me because the night before, I had a dream. I was somewhere I had never been before, but it was cold; it was my house; Robby was there in the backyard. I was dressed in a nursing uniform, and I was genuinely happy; I was at peace. I walked outside where Robby was; there were two green apple trees; I walked up to one of the trees and grabbed an apple and took a bite, and then I grabbed another one and put it in my pocket. I turned and looked at Robby and said, "I am going to save that one for later." I went and kissed his cheek and then turned and left for work.

Wow. I just stood there thinking, *Is this God? Is He real? Is He trying to tell me that I am not poison and that I am supposed to be with Robby?* I have been fed so many lies that I thought to be truths, and suddenly, I am faced with a new truth, His truth. What do I do with this? My heart softened at the thought. I looked at Robby, and I said, "I love you, and I always will, but sometimes love just isn't enough." I got into the truck, and we just talked. As we went through the motions and realized where we went wrong and that not being obedient to God led us to this place. We made a decision in that car at that moment that we would try one more time. We knew we owed it to each other and to God to give us a fair shot. We decided it was time to move to Tennessee.

Chapter 28

2016: THE MOVE TO TENNESSEE

"I will bring the blind by a way they did not know; I will lead them in paths they have not known. I will make darkness light before them, And crooked places straight. These things I will do for them, And not forsake them."

—Isaiah 42:16 (NKJV)

It is amazing how fast things can happen when you say yes to God! While sitting in the U-Haul and with the truck loaded down with all of our belongings, it is crazy to think that just two weeks before, we were going to get a divorce. Our house and boats sold in a matter of days, and we had a handful of cash, and I accepted a position in Chattanooga, Tennessee. And now, here we sit with the house in our rearview mirror, and as we drive away, I am silently leaving the memories that have haunted me right where they belong! I can hear my screams getting more distant the further down the road we go.

There is an anticipation in the air mixed with a sweet

sadness, knowing Robby is leaving the place he loves and grew up in for us. Maybe there is a small part of me that is also sad because this has been such a big part of who I am for so long. What if we don't make it, what if we hate it, what if I can't heal? There are so many uncertainties, but we know what God said, and this time, we will obey. We are going to a place we have never been and a place where we do not know anyone, and in our hearts, we know it is going to be okay one way or another.

We arrive to our new home and start to unload our stuff. My children are being such good sports, trying to set up their rooms and make a new place for themselves. No one is complaining or giving us a hard time, and if anyone has teenagers, you know that must be God. Our first night there was amazing. There was peace and smiles. Everything fit perfectly, and we knew we did the right thing.

Unfortunately, things didn't stay in the honeymoon phase. About a week in, Robby's pain and my pain began to seep through. It was then I realized my past and brokenness would follow me everywhere I went. I was losing hope. I hated who I had become, I hated my past, and I loathed that no matter what I did, it would always be there. Robby started digging deeper into God with doors opening to new avenues and new God relationships, while I struggled with self-hate and old patterns of locking myself away to cope.

It was during this time I became out of control; I was anxious and irrational, and I would wake up with night sweats. I didn't trust Robby; I would be so mean and accusatory toward him. He could never catch a break. I would attack him. When I think back, I really don't know how he stayed. I was destroying him with my words and with my actions. This was my breaking point; I knew I couldn't take much more; I thought of death often. I just didn't feel like I had any other choice. Something was off; it was more than just the normal brokenness I have dealt with throughout the years. It was over-the-top, uncontrollable, extreme emotions.

I was at work one day, and I was walking around, feeling like my insides were trying to escape out of my body. My heart felt weird. I was sweaty. A coworker asked me if I was feeling okay; I said, "No, I feel strange." She had me sit down and hooked me up to the heart monitors in our unit, and my heart was beating over 170 beats per minute. That started me on the path of loads of medical tests and some diagnostic procedures. I was put on beta blockers to slow my heart rate while I waited for my results. I went into the doctor's office and was told I had Graves' disease and was in a thyroid storm and needed surgery ASAP. I left the office and went to my car and cried my eyes out. Not only was my life spinning out of control, but now my health was too. I picked up the phone, and I called Robby and just sobbed. He, like always, was the rock I needed; he was so calm and soothing and loving despite the hell I had put him through previously. Being the man of wisdom he is, he stated he would come pick me up and we would make an appointment with an endocrinologist and get a second opinion. My nerves settled enough for me to drive home and reflect over what had led me to this point.

I did my research and, after much searching, found an endocrinologist in my area with good reviews. The endocrinologist ran his own test and asked me to come into his office the following week.

When he came into the room, he gently looked me over and said, "So, when was the first time you endured a trauma?"

I was shocked and stunned. I said, "Excuse me."

He said, "You have the antibodies for both Hashimoto's and Graves' disease. Your antibodies are so high I believe you have had Hashimoto's since childhood and that a lack of treatment led to Graves'.

I then proceeded to ask, "What does trauma have to do with either?"

He then looked me in the face and stated, "There are recent studies that suggest autoimmune disorders are closely linked to trauma. So, I need to know when you first experienced trauma."

Then, all of a sudden, it hit me: my body was attacking itself. Wow! All the self-hate I have felt over the years, and my body finally turned on itself. I looked at him with irritation, and I said, "Well, which time do you want to know about?"

He shook his head in acknowledgment and didn't press the issue; my reply was all he needed.

I left that office armed with new knowledge that if this could happen from trauma, surely it could be helped and reversed if I could just figure out a way to reverse the self-hate. The next year, I was on a mission for healing, for forgiveness, to be made whole once and for all. I tried everything; I was prayed for, went through deliverance, changed my diet, and while I was feeling better, healing wasn't coming. I was still triggered easily, still having bursts of irrationality. I was absolutely impossible to live with; nothing was working. No matter what spiritual hoop I went through, I was still this broken, sick little girl suffering with bitterness and self-hate, which affected every area of my life. I needed God to intervene, and I needed Him to intervene fast before my family walked away from me or before I ended it all for good so I couldn't hurt anyone ever again. I was desperate and ready for whatever God had for me. It was time, and I was waiting with my arms wide open, desperate for His healing touch.

Chapter 29

2018: MY GOD MOMENT SEPTEMBER

"For if you forgive men their trespasses, your heavenly Father will also forgive you."

—Matthew 6:14 (NKJV)

"Oh my God, are you serious right now? I can't believe you are not answering the phone." I slam the phone down in anger as Robby has not answered my call for the fourth time in ten minutes. I don't care if he is at church; I don't care what he is doing. Isn't his service to me first? Am I not his wife? I will show him. I pick my phone back up and send a text, saying not to come home if he can't answer me. I scroll through my phone and see this is the fifteenth message I have sent him in the last thirty minutes. I don't care if this is absurd. What is absurd is putting other people before your wife. What if I was dying, or one of the kids were hurt? Doesn't he care about us?

I grab the remote in a fury and sit back in the recliner. I am done; I am not ever talking to him again; we are done once and for all. I sigh and take a deep breath, turn the television on, and look for something to watch. Flipping through the movies on my Prime, I see movies I have seen a million times; nothing looks good. I am too aggravated to search for something. Then suddenly, a movie appears as I scroll. *Oh yes, this will do the trick.* It's a very controversial movie about God, and I am so all about controversy right now. I am in a stirring the pot kinda mood. I sit back and press play with a big smile on my face, hoping this movie is as bad as others say it is; get some more fuel for the flame.

It isn't long after it starts, I feel a bit of unease as it seems to be about an abduction, rape, and murder of a little girl, all huge triggers for me. My alarm bells are going off; I am not happy anymore; I am triggered and sad. Why do people have to do such horrible things to people? Why does God allow it? Where is the justice? I start to get furious as the movie plays on; my anger toward the perpetrator, toward God, and suddenly, an anger toward myself rears its ugly head. There are too many emotions running through my body, and I am just about to shut it off and shut down. Protection mode is right on the edge, and I can feel it creeping in.

That's when it happened: all of a sudden, the father is

brought into a place behind a waterfall and faced with a decision; he is presented with two of his children, and after he is told of the bad they have done, he is asked to choose who is punished, who goes to hell. And as the tears stream down my face, I can see things from a different perspective, a different light. Hurt people hurt people, and where does the cycle stop? We are all God's children, and He wants us all redeemed. I sat there thinking of all the people who ever hurt me, and for the first time in my life, I was trying to think what hell could they have gone through that made them the people who made such bad decisions. Then I thought, *What if they are in heaven when this is all said and done?* Then I thought, *Do I deserve heaven?* I know I have tortured the ones I loved and withheld my love from the ones who needed it most. Then, all of a sudden, I felt a warmth and a peace. It felt as if God was wrapping me in His arms, and I just sobbed and sobbed.

Thinking back on this moment brings fresh tears to my eyes, as this is the moment I realized that God loves all His creations, and He died for us all. We all have a will and ultimately make our own decisions, sometimes even sick, horrible decisions, but that does not change His love for us. He wants us all healed and whole and with Him for eternity, and He doesn't want to choose one of us over the other as He wants us all redeemed. That was mind-blowing to me. For the first time, I was armed with the truth that He loves us that much. The first thing that came from this revelation was that, for the first time ever, I was able to forgive myself. For not being everything I was called to be, for falling short so many times, for disobeying His Word, for harboring anger and bitterness toward the people I believed deserved it, for allowing myself to be in situations that ultimately harmed my body and my soul, and the biggest of all, for not speaking out when I had a chance and save the body and soul of another because I was too afraid to do what was right.

There I was, sitting in my living room weeping, my soul healing, my mind being transformed. I was not jumping through any hoops; in fact, my heart was just in a dark place before this moment, angry and bitter. But God had a plan all along; He knew the moment and the method, and it was not the normal cookie-cutter way that you often hear about in testimonies. It was just me and Him in my living room, and without a single prayer, He showed up and showed me the very thing it would take to heal my wounded soul. It was my very own one-of-a-kind balm of Gilead blended just for me, just for this moment.

I had been searching and doing the things I had been instructed to do for months to find my physical healing, but on that day, God gave me something I needed even more but didn't realize it. He healed my soul, not my body. He picked up all the shattered pieces and put me back together. It's funny how we can go on a search for what we think we need or do the things other people think we need to do to become what they think we should be, but in the end, God shows up and does what He knows in His glorious power is just what we need at that time. I will never be the same again; I have been forever changed with just one moment from the Father.

I now know what I must do; I must go and tell all who will listen what the Lord has done for me. It is where my freedom and the freedom of others will come from. I will not be afraid to speak the truth and to show the love of God to the people who need it the most, no matter how uncomfortable it feels or how hard it may be. I know I have a long way to go, but this is my first step into walking out the obedience of God and finding my way back to my voice!

Chapter 30

THERE IS A HOPE

"For whatever things were written before were written for our learning, that we through the patience and comfort of the Scriptures might have hope."

—Romans 15:4 (NKJV)

As I sit here today writing the final chapter of this book, I am contemplating what to leave you with. I would love to tell you I am a completely healed spirit, soul, and body, but that would be a lie; I am not perfect. While I am by no means the person I was before, I still battle sickness; I still have triggers, although, I will say, much less than before; they are still there nonetheless. I still struggle with my emotions, but what I can tell you is that I am making progress and that there is a hope! My life has changed in so many ways in this past year. I am so happy I can finally see what's on the other side of my pain; there is hope, joy, and a peace that passes all understanding. I am no longer sitting and waiting for the bottom to fall out or for another trauma to happen. I am getting up and taking action. I will no longer sit in silence and allow the devil to annihilate me anymore; I will no longer sit back and be in agreement with the lies of my past. I am whole! I am healed! I am more than a conqueror! I am the head and not the tail! I have the power of God deep inside of me, just waiting for me to tap into it and be all that I have been called to be! What an amazing gift.

One thing I have learned in all of this is we have to own our piece of this puzzle. I know for me, in the beginning, I was an innocent child deserving of none of it. But as I got older, I was playing with fire. I am not saying that anyone deserves to be raped; for that, I am innocent. But I put myself in many compromising situations and behaved in a way that wasn't pure. Searching for freedom any way I could get it. Fast forward to my more recent years and the trauma I had endured. I was mean and nasty to my loved ones, torturing them every chance I got and using my trauma as a crutch for my bad behavior, and that is just not okay. We have to learn to take ownership of our actions and refuse to torture the ones we love in the name of trauma. Our family deserves better than that. We have to run to the Father and ask Him to help us heal and teach us how to treat our loved ones with compassion and not as if they are the enemy. Yahweh is just and will teach you how to be the person you were always meant to be without damaging your children, your husband, or anyone else that is within your family. We have to seek out our healing every day.

There are so many things you can do if you are trapped in a shattered, trauma-filled past if you want to loosen the chains and finally reach your destiny full of hope and freedom. They will be, in no particular order: Make a choice to turn to jump off the hamster wheel cycle and turn your eye towards Yeshua. If there is any rift between you and God, make it right right now. Take the time to speak to Him and wait for the reply. Worship twenty-four hours a day, now that is not just the music but worship Him in everything, with your whole heart. Let every action you do be in worship. It is not about us; after all, it's about Him. I personally, in the beginning of this journey to my voice, would keep earbuds in my ears twenty-four seven; during the day, I would listen to worship or teaching while doing life throughout the day, and at night, I would listen to biblical words of affirmation while I slept and this is when I noticed the most significant change. Find anyone who needs help, and help them. I find helping others helps to get the focus off of me and onto what is really important. I would recommend anyone who is full of trauma and is having a problem with triggers and is unable to control their emotions to get a hold of Rebecca King's Soul Fast teaching; it really helps you to gain perspective and put the emotions where they belong. And last but not least of all is, parents, you have to teach your children to be bold and brave and to never surrender their voice. Children are particularly vulnerable due to their lack of emotional maturity and the inability to process what is happening and how to deal with it. So, parents, always keep your lines of communication open; let your children know they can come to you for anything and that nothing will ever change the love you have for them.

For the first time in my life, I can notice a real change in me, my heart, and my actions. I am not looking for validation from anyone but God. I am not trying to find a way out; I am facing my life with the boldness I once had as a child. It is so scary and beautiful all at the same time. God has restored my marriage and is showing me ever so gently that I do belong with Robby, always have, and always will. I am so grateful for all my life's lessons; they have brought me to this turning point and made me who I am today.

Now, it's time to stop giving the enemy your voice. Take it back! The Bible says in Matthew 11:12 (NKJV), "And from the days of John the Baptist until now the kingdom of heaven suffers violence, and the violent take it by force." We are not to sit back and let the enemy win. We have to pick up the Word of God, read it, and get to know it intimately; it is one of the greatest weapons we have as followers of Yeshua (Jesus). Then, we need to start opening up our mouths and telling the truths of our past; let your testimony be heard loud and clear. In Revelations 12:11 (NKJV), it says, "And they overcame him by the blood of the Lamb and by the word of their testimony, and they did not love their lives to the death." This is why the Word of God is so important in our lives; it has all the answers we will ever need!

So, if you are like me and you have had to endure pain and trauma that you were never created to endure, forgive the people who hurt you, forgive God, and never forget to forgive yourself. It is time to pick up your sword, the Word of God, read it, know it inside and out; it was given to you as a guide, begin to worship in everything that you do, start waring in prayer, and find someone who is lost and hurting and help them. And I promise you will not be disappointed; just watch Yahweh move.

I pray my words have given you a hope that you can overcome your past and the knowledge that the trauma you have experienced does not have to define who you are; the only thing that can do that is God; you have a purpose, a reason that you were brought into this world. It says so in Jeremiah 29:11 (NKJV): "For I know the thoughts that I think toward you, says the Lord, thoughts of peace and not of evil, to give you a future and a hope." Isn't that amazing? It says it right there in the Word. I love you all so much, and I want all of God's people healed and whole.

Let's pray.

Dear heavenly Father,

I pray that You touch the person who is reading this and anyone who has suffered traumas in their lifetime, let them know that You love them so much, show them the areas that need healing, and give them the strength they need to walk this healing out. I pray for grace and mercy as they are learning this new way of life with You! Let them know it is okay if they mess up or don't get it right—this is a process, and it took a long time to get the way they are now—and that sometimes you have to walk through the many layers before you start to notice fewer and fewer triggers. Fill them with the Holy Spirit and set fire to their bones so that they are not satisfied until they have all you have to offer. Draw them into the garden for a deeper communion with you. We love You, Father, and we are eternally grateful for this life You have given us; help us not to take it for granted. We love You, Abba!

Amen!

Printed in the USA
CPSIA information can be obtained
at www.ICGtesting.com
LVHW011930070224
771125LV00008B/139